FOGO DE CHÃO

GAUCHO TRADITION GAINS WORLDWIDE STATUS

FOGO DE CHÃO®
CHURRASCARIA
BRAZILIAN STEAKHOUSE

In a building with a galant façade, restored according to the original architectural standards, in the heart of Washington, DC, only a short distance from the White House, one of the branches of the United States Fogo de Chão (fo-go dèe shoun, freely translated as open fire on the ground or campfire) steakhouses has been operating since 2005.

In an environment that merges the local scene with typically Brazilian components, the symbols of the gaucho tradition are combined with the American capital's characteristic features. Waiters wearing bombachas, the gaucho baggy pants, boots, blue shirt and red scarf, mingle harmoniously with United States congress members, democrats and republicans, diplomats and tourists from all over the world, who come in search of the authentic churrasco, or Brazilian gaucho-style barbecue. In this intense fusion of cultures, a intriguing power ritual takes place, in conversations that proceed in a varied universe of accents and languages.

The Washington branch is part of the chain of sixteen Brazilian steakhouses established from coast to coast, recognized in the United States for the flavor of its meats, for its exclusive products and the differentiated service that has captivated Americans.

Fogo de Chão unveiled its flag in the United States early in 1997, in Dallas, with a firm commitment to conquer the American public. The trailblazers of this campaign relied on the strength of a united and brave team, with an unshakable disposition to play down the distance from home and face up to the unexpected problems, which were many early on in the game.

The willingness, professionalism and dedication of this team ensured the attainment of the goal – the brand was implemented relatively quickly in the United States, and today the Fogo de Chão name is recognized as the synonym of the renowned gaucho-style churrasco, which has ensured the chain's continued growth and the winning over of an immense legion of customers and friends.

In 2005, Fogo de Chão opened in Washington, D.C., installed in a stylish address, close to the White House, on Pennsylvania Avenue

Integrated into the neighborhood in an area that attracts daily visitors in the federal capital, Fogo de Chão has been operating in Brasília since 2007

In Brazil's capital, a city of worldwide importance and the geopolitical Center of South America, the Fogo de Chão brand has been active since 2007 and, just as in the United States capital, the steakhouse is the venue for the meeting of diplomats, foreign tourists, entrepreneurs and members of a broad and diversified national political universe, which in a large communion of gastronomical interest enjoys the meats prepared and served according to the chain's traditional standard.

The chain's arrival in Brasília was received with great enthusiasm by the market, the press and opinion makers, thanks to the good image of the other branches operating in Brazil. But its success can also be attributed to the cosmopolitan nature reigning in Brasília, which gathers people from all over the country and the world, many of whom are merely passing through the city, because Brasília is the temporary residence of Brazilians and foreigners that reside there in order to perform roles in the political, corporate business and diplomatic representation areas.

Since its opening, the Brasília branch of the Fogo de Chão chain has been a point of attraction and convergence of a broad public, serving as the stage and scene of important political and corporate business decisions.

Fogo de Chão is a Brazilian enterprise with roots planted in the State of Rio Grande do Sul, but with its eyes permanently focused on the world and the great possibilities for expansion that are unveiled each day.

True to the commitment undertaken thirty years ago by its founders, the company will remain attentive to new opportunities for growth, both within and outside of Brazil, in order to ensure returns and stability to its stockholders, partners and contributors.

FOGO DE CHÃO – GAUCHO TRADITION GAINS WORLDWIDE STATUS

© 2010

SMS Editora Ltda.

Rua Pamplona, 1119 - Conjunto 73

01405-001 - São Paulo - SP

5511 3289-8133

premio@premioeditorial.com.br

Publisher: Marino Lobello

Research and writing: Aline Sasahara

Research in United States of America: Jorge Tarquini

Graphic design: Gerson Silva Reis Jr

Edition: Aline Sasahara and Cássia Fragata

Editing: Angela Mendes/ Informart Arte e Design Ltda

English translation: Peter Galsgaard

English proofreading: Fernanda Santos

Graphic production: Samuel Lincon Silvério

Operational suport: Moacir Aparecido Rosa da Silva

Printing and finishing: Ipsis Gráfica e Editora

17

The paternal home,
the beginning of everything

43

Fogo de Chão
embraces Brazil

77

Fogo de Chão
conquers America

Showcased in all the chain's restaurants, the authentic *gaucho churrasco* for your enjoyment

This book records a story that we began to write more than 30 years ago, when we couldn't possibly imagine the future size of the undertaking that we were to build.

Here are set down important facts that marked the journey of Fogo de Chão, besides personal and affectionate memories that emerged in the course of the work.

We have come this far because we believed in the business that we were building, although we wouldn't have managed it without the help and confidence of many people, of our parents and siblings, of our friends, partners and customers, and particularly of our dedicated team of coworkers who have helped us with their labor and suggestions, enabling the small churrascaria in Porto Alegre to grow and conquer the world.

And, in addition, nothing would have been possible without the understanding of our dear wives, who were able to grasp the extent of our dream and who encouraged us to proceed, even in the face of the limitations of time and constant absences from our homes.

We are today a group that employs more than 2,000 people in 22 restaurants in Brazil and the United States, and we are continuously expanding our business, making available far and wide the flavor and tradition of the true gaucho churrasco, which is recognized as one of the acclaimed features of the Brazilian culture.

To one and all our sincere gratitude.

Jair and Arri Coser

Chapter 1

Work was always part of the Coser family's day-to-day routine. In the immensity of the Vale do Taquari, in the Serra Gaúcha[1], activity in the home began early and there was no lack of tasks for each one of the seven children of Mr. Ângelo and Mrs. Leontina. Work in the field, and taking care of the calves, pigs and sheep left no room for laziness. Work was blended with fun

The paternal home,
the beginning of everything

and games that occurred in a dreamlike scenario: an unending succession of mountains with the River Jacaré flowing alongside the road.

The Serra Gaúcha received with arms wide open the families arriving from Europe in order to escape the crisis there, seeking new opportunities in this new country

_____

[1] A mountainous region in the west of the State of Rio Grande do Sul, in southern Brazil, principally colonized by Italian and German immigrants.

The yard of the house where the brothers Coser
played and pretended that it was the world

A road that *nonno* (grandfather) Pedro, who also lived in the house, walked while carrying the hoe and singing, teaching the children songs from old Italy which were then sung at the end of the working day, on the porch of the house, sometimes accompanied by the guitar of grandson Jair:

> *Dalla Italia noi siamo partiti*
> *Siamo partiti col nostro onore*
> *Trentasei giorni di macchina e vapore,*

> *e nella Merica noi siamo arriva'.*
> *Merica, Merica, Merica,*
> *cossa saràlo 'sta Merica?*
> *Merica, Merica, Merica,*
> *un bel mazzolino di fior.*[2]

And with stories that brought to mind perseverance, conquests and sacrifice, *nonno* caused the emergence among the youths of values such as courage, an enterprising spirit and respect. Values that

---

[2] A section of the song composed in 1875, part of the Italian folklore, which became a sort of hymn of those who migrated from Italy to America. *(From Italy we left / We left with our honor / Thirty-six days on a steamboat, /And in America we arrived. / America, America, America, / What is this America? / America, America, America, / A lovely nosegay of flowers.)*

were to mark the life's journey of each one of those children and would delineate the character of Fogo de Chão (fo-go dèe shoun, freely translated as open fire on the ground or campfire). These were memories from the time in which the first Coser—together with so many other immigrant Italian families running away from the crisis in the Old World— made the great crossing and established themselves in the region, ready to embark on a new life in the new land. Determined to plant their roots in the Brazilian soil and there raise their children — sons and daughters of Rio Grande do Sul.

It proved necessary to cultivate previously unexplored land, open tracks through the forest, build houses with their own hands, and plant in order to harvest and live from the fruit of this continued labor. To the songs from old Italy were added the tunes of Rio Grande. In the authentic gaucho dwelling, discussion of the day's activities took place within the circle of the mate infusion drinkers.

The unified family came out winning and thus remained. While the maternal grandfather lived in the Coser's own house, the father of Mr. Ângelo, *nonno* Daniel, lived in the neighboring home and also closely followed the growth of his children's children. As all of them were neighbors, they would often organize a

In the idyllic landscape of the Serra Gaúcha, the Coser family planted its Brazilian roots. Above, Leontina and Angelo Coser

Everything that was consumed in their day-to-day living was produced right there. Ranging from the meals to the blankets woven from sheep's wool, from wine to clothing. The simple life was reflected in the dedication to work. Work in which even the children were involved involved, blending work with games

collective effort to deal with a heavy task at the home of one of the group's members or in someone else's field.

And everything that was consumed was taken from the earth and processed right there. Thus, from the wheat harvested they made flour which was stacked in sacks, laid tightly one on top of the other so as to better preserve the product. And with that flour they kneaded the dough to make bread eaten with *chimia*[3], cooked for hours in large vats, leaving the smell of fruit and sweets in the air. Rice, beans, potatoes, corn, everything was obtained through their labor. Even clothes were handsewn by the women. Father would bring fabrics from town, and the sewing, like the songs sung in a chorus, would last into the night or would fill up the time on rainy days, while the men shucked corn in the barn or worked at other tasks that might be done while it rained outside. Even the thick quilts, essential to face the Highland's cold, were made right there, with sheep's wool, which after the shearing was washed in the river, then stretched out to dry in the sun, beaten and then carded, turning fluffy like cotton. Part of it was packed and sold. Organization was essential so that nothing might be lacking. This Mr. Ângelo had learned in the army and applied daily with his "labor team."

In this environment of considerable dedication, fresh air

---

[3] *Chimia* is the name given in the region to jam spread on bread. *Chimiê* or *chimíer* is an adaptation of the German expression *schimiere*, which means to "smear, grease," created by the descendants of Germans who live in the south of Brazil.

and companionship, the brothers Jair and Arri were born and raised. Arri, his name wrongly recorded by the registrar with two r's, recalls nostalgically the fishing excursions on the Jacaré River, on which he and Jair were accompanied by his grandfather, but one at a time, so that the talking between the *guris*[4] would not frighten away the fish: carp, wolf fish, catfish, mudcat and lambari. It was in the waters of the Jacaré River that Mr. Ângelo taught the boys to swim. Because to be allowed to fish in the river, they would first have to learn how to fend for themselves in the water.

It was along this friendly river, following the dirt road's curves, entirely bordered by trees, that the children walked to school over a distance of roughly 1 km, accompanied by their teacher, Santina Lorence. In order to be closer to her work, Mrs. Santina was welcomed into the Coser household. Children from everywhere would join them as they walked along the Road forming a group of almost 25 as they arrived at the Charrua School, the only option for study provided to the community's children. The rest of the time was split between work and play.

Churrasco (gaucho-style barbecue) in the home of the Coser family? Always! Every month Mr. Ângelo would slaughter livestock and, whether it was a pig, sheep or bull, he would quickly prepare the fire to roast the meat. As there was no refrigera-

At the top, the boy Arri with his parents, in their Sunday clothes. Above, the family pictured on a Holiday

---

[4] The expression that refers to a boy, a child, in the State of Rio Grande do Sul.

Fare l'América: Italians plant an Italy in Brazil

'Survetinho, survetón, survetinho de limón, quem não tem o dez tostón não toma sorvetón', 'O formagio! Olha o formagio!' 'A tostón o pedaço! Melanzia barata! Come, bebe e lava a cara', 'Ô pimenta!', 'Batata assata al forn! ("Small ice cream, large ice cream, lemon ice cream, no ice cream for those who don't have 10 cents," "The cheese! Here's the cheese!" "At a dime a piece! "Cheap watermelon! Eat, drink and wash your face," "Here's pepper!" "Oven-baked potato!")

The hawking of vendors, heavy with the dialects of Italy, echoed across the streets of São Paulo, in a veritable urban symphony. This was the time when the *Fanfulla* newspaper circulated in the streets, at one time being the city's largest daily publication. The Italians, after all, represented 57.4% of those who immigrated to Brazil, between the years of 1880 and 1904, when the country still presented large areas yet unpopulated, and had to adapt to life without slave labor. The Association for the Promotion of Immigration, established in 1886, in its first three years of activity was responsible for the arrival in Brazil of 17,856 European families.

In Italy, meanwhile, the low wages, high taxes and the lack of land available for cultivation, were some of the factors that led its people to seek a more rewarding future in overseas lands. The illiteracy rate was high, and epidemic diseases threatened families, as a result of the abandonment and deep poverty that marked the recently unified Italy.

Brazil emerged as a welcoming center, a land of no ills, a land of plenty, but very far away. A letter addressed to the "friend and settler" circulated throughout Italy, seeking to convince people to emigrate to Brazil, providing for the labor needs of the large farmers in the State of São Paulo and for the colonization of the unpopulated lands.

Before this large migratory movement, Italians had already settled in the State of Rio Grande do Sul, having arrived in ships that docked in Porto Alegre, or in ships arriving from Rio de Janeiro and São Paulo. The immigrants came from several regions, spoke different dialects and brought along varied cultural customs with them.

The first large challenge was to survive the long ocean crossing, under very precarious conditions lacking in comfort,

hygiene and nourishment, with the heart already full of longing and the mind plagued by doubts about what lay ahead. Then, the road to their parcel of land was opened by means of machetes. And there they had to start from nothing. Everything they needed for their sustenance had to be grown on the farm. This caused them to be diversified in their agricultural output, a feature that persists in these regions that were colonized in this fashion.

Once settled, many immigrants called on their family and friends to come to the new country as well, which was to become the homeland of their sons and grandchildren, future inhabitants of that part of Brazil. There were frequent contacts with other groups of European settlers who were also undergoing the same cultural adjustment process: Frenchmen, Poles and, principally, Germans.

The difference in languages was a hindrance to be overcome, since communication with the Brazilians was fundamental. Among the different dialects, that of Venice stands out, in the formulation of a sort of general dialect. But the *brasiliano*, or an *Italianized* Portuguese, gained increasing presence among the immigrants, distancing them from their roots. Thus, the role of the grandparents and great-grandparents was fundamental in the conveying of the traditions of their land of origin to their descendants.

The Coser family arrived in Brazil in 1887, having come from Trento. The parents, Mrs. Leontina and Mr. Ângelo, met each other in the Gaucho Highlands and there they formed a family, created and organized according to the purest gaucho spirit. A good number of their sons continue to work the land, making of that region a small piece of Italy in Brazil.

In need of workers that might replace the existing slave labor, particularly in the large coffee plantations, and of families capable of colonizing the still uninhabited areas of its vast territory, the Brazilian government implemented an intense policy of encouraging immigration, as of the 1880s

tor, time was of the essence, making the most of the animal slaughtered, the family would prepare stuffed meat items: sausages, salami and coppa. The adults would concentrate on this work, while the children, from an early age, had lots of fun roasting beefsteaks. And besides this great family event, on nearly every weekend there would be church festivities and the entire community would gather. The bull would be slaughtered, divided into small pieces and the families would then place their orders before the Mass began: 4 skewers, or 5, so that nobody would go without. While the Mass was celebrated in the church's interior the smell of the marvelous *churrasco* enticed the people out on the street. A veritable feast!

From the welcoming Serra Gaúcha to the immensity of Brazil

Jair and Arri always looked ahead. No matter how healthy life was in their region, the two brothers were thinking of following the journey of so many other youths who had left to work in São Paulo, Rio de Janeiro, and Curitiba, the great majority as a waiter in a *churrascaria*, or gaucho-style steakhouse. But even though the *churrasco* was part of the daily routine of these young sons and daughters of the Serra

Jair was the first son of Mr. Angelo and Mrs. Leontina to leave home. With his mind set on a more promising future, he left the paternal home and entered the seminary

Gaúcha, to take the first step in a journey headed far from their father's home was not an easy move.

Jair saw in the seminary the possibility of expanding his world beyond those mountains. Father Giocondo, their parish priest, realizing the young man's enterprising spirit, provided the encouragement. And, at the age of 15, the fourth son of the Coser family journeyed to Sacred Heart of Jesus Marist Seminary, at Arroio do Meio, 60 km from home. To the family, an unimaginable distance: 2 to 3 hours by bus or truck.

Arri remained on the land, or better, thought about how to escape from tilling the fields.

The sisters relate and he himself admits that working with the hoe was never his preference. It was common for him and the youngest sister, his favorite companion for playing games, to break the tool's handle so that "they would be unable to work". And everything would turn into a toy in the hands of Arri: the bucket with which he got the milk, the lid of the vat in which the *chimia* cooked, the seeds that he was supposed to plant. He used to dream of being a pilot of fighter planes engaged in military training, which would fly low over their house, always at the same hour and this would additionally provoke the boy's curiosity about "the world out there."

Added to the lack of work opportunities, there was also the fact that the family's land was no longer sufficient for everybody. Besides Jair, Arri and the brothers, there were the uncles and

At the age of 14, still a youngster, Arri Coser left the Serra Gaúcha to don a waiter's uniform at a churrascaria in Aparecida do Norte. Above, the Coser family, ever together

cousins, who weren't few, and the land had been gradually split up. Little or practically nothing was left for the younger family members.

Thus, at the age of 14, Arri took his first great step: he left the Serra Gaúcha with his mind full of dreams, several shirts made by his sisters and a knot in his throat. He went on to "conquer Brazil," following in the older brother's brave steps. The protection of the paternal home was left behind. He headed for Aparecida do Norte, a town in the State of São Paulo, famous for receiving every day thousands of pilgrims at its basilica. And although his parents had long known Mr. Cestári, who took charge of the young man and gave him a job at his restaurant, the mother's heart grieved. Mrs. Leontina and his sisters

Feeling entirely confident, Jair and Arri Coser left their small town, lodged in the landscape of Rio Grande do Sul, in order to establish their own business

did not believe that this development would work out, that the boy, who had been pampered by everybody, would be able to remain distant from his home for a long while.

The youngest sister, longing for her playful companion, recalls that at the end of the day, already having bathed, she sat looking out the window until she would give up: "I think he won't come today. It's already dark…" And, in fact, nearly three years went by before the brother returned home.

Jair had also left the seminary. Having come of age, he had already awaited Arri's arrival in Aparecida over the past six months. The 60 km that had separated him from the warmth of the paternal home were now a good deal more than 1,000 km.

He worked at the establishment of Mr. Cestári, at the Churras-caria Rio Grandense, where Arri was to become the "juice-serving boy." It so happened that the boss, on a trip to Rio de Janeiro, was charmed by the city's popular fruit-juice bars and decided to bring the novelty back to Aparecida. He built a small house right beside the *churrascaria* where, for a few months, the young Arri prepared liters and liters of natural fruit juices.

The Rio Grandense steakhouse was situated at the Poço das Pedras Pintadas (Well of the Painted Stones), where all the buses loaded with pilgrims would stop. There was a veritable crowd of people. One sunday, when Jair had already been pro-moted to night manager, a customer invited him to work at one of his two restaurants in Rio de Janeiro, located at the Ilha do Governador international airport. The wage offered was tempt-ing: twice as much as he earned at Aparecida.

Above, Jair Coser, young and resolute

Jair was unable to refuse the offer and he journeyed to Rio, a place about which he knew nothing and where he knew nobody. He spent the first night at the airport's bathroom. Then, on the ad-vice of his colleagues at the restaurant, he obtained lodgings close to his job, which didn't last longer than a week: Jair soon discov-ered that there was a *churrascaria* in town owned by gauchos. He went there, asked for a job and was hired. "Oásis" was the name of the establishment which belonged to a large business organization, also with origins in the interior of Rio Grande do Sul.

Six months after his admission, the restaurant's owners opened a branch in Niterói and Jair invited his brother to work

As he was still a minor, in order to work away from home, Arri left the Serra Gaúcha under Jair's responsibility

at the new place. He went to Aparecida to get his brother since, Arri being a minor, he was not allowed to travel on his own. Jair was then 20 years old but possessed considerable responsibility: in addition to the role of brother he also took on that of guardian, since Arri was only 15 years old when he arrived in Niterói with his mind full of ideas. The example provided at the paternal home and the gregarious and companionable nature of the people of Rio Grande do Sul would ensure the success of this mission. The two would proceed together, would grow and extend the fruits of their work across Brazil, covering the entire country. Dishwasher, busboy, waiter, assistant *churrasqueiro*, *churrasqueiro* chef. The brothers Jair and Arri Coser worked at these and other jobs during the beginnings of their professional journey, always driven by the dream of owning their own business. This meant intense learning, not only with respect to the business itself but also in regard to the importance of human relations in the day-to-day work. Each skewer prepared, each dish served, was part of the building of this dream. In a short while the brothers headed for São Conrado and Botafogo, in the Marvelous City [5].

There life wasn't all that different: work and then more work. Once in a while they would take in a movie or go to the beach. Their lodgings were modest and they took their meals at

[5] Botafogo and São Conrado are districts of the City of Rio de Janeiro, made famous because of its lovely geography as the Cidade Maravilhosa (Marvelous City). Like Niterói, the city of Rio is situated in the State of Rio de Janeiro.

ESTADO DO RIO GRANDE DO SUL
P O D E R   J U D I C I Á R I O

ALVARÁ DE LICENÇA PARA VIAJAR

O EXMO. SR. DR. ARNO WERLANG, MM. JUIZ
ADJUNTO DESTA COMARCA DE ENCANTADO, ES
TADO DO RIO GRANDE DO SUL, ETC.-

Atendendo ao requerimento de ANGELO COZER,
brasileiro, casado, agricultor,,residente e domiciliado na Vila
de Relvado-Encantado-RS., A U T O R I Z O seu filho menor ARRI
COZER, nascido a 20 de março de 1962, a viajar em companhia de
seu irmão JAIR COSER, maior, até a cidade do Rio de Janeiro, -
onde o referido menor pretende trabalhar.

DADO E PASSADO nesta cidade de Encantado,-
aos trinta e um dias do mês de agosto do ano de mil novecentos/
e setenta e sete (31/08/1977). Eu, _____ , Oficial Judicial o datilografei e subscrevi.

Plinio José de Adelle
SERVIÇO JUDICIAL

A R N O   W E R L A N G

JUIZ ADJUNTO

2ª VARA

The *churrasco*, born in the pampas

Introduced in the territory of Rio Grande do Sul in the 17th century, when the region was fought over between the empires of Spain, with headquarters in Buenos Aires, on the Plate River, and of Portugal, headquartered in Rio de Janeiro, cattle became the area's source of great wealth.

Based on the Treaty of Tordesillas, signed in 1493, an imaginary line divided the world recently discovered as a result of the voyages of Christopher Columbus between the two kingdoms and, under this division, the territory in which Rio Grande do Sul is placed today theoretically belonged to the Spaniards.

Around this time, priests from the Company of Jesus crossed the Uruguay River and established themselves in the region as the Seven People of the Missions, Jesuit villages were founded with the aim of converting the native peoples to the Christian faith. When the missions were destroyed by the Portuguese in 1768, an immense number of cattle were abandoned, giving rise to large wild herds, which ran freely across the gaucho pampas[1].

Cattle drivers and muleteers, called *tropeiros*, who in addition to driving large herds also transported on the back of mules products to market in the villages and towns that emerged across the country's interior, also brought along news and new customs. In the long journeys they faced bad weather and were guided by the rivers where there were no roads. The abundance of cattle made that region into a strategic stop for these travelers, allowing them to rest and satisfy their hunger, roasting the meat on the fire that also gave them heat throughout the night. This was the *churrasco*.

Later, the cattle fatteners who in the winter season drove the cattle to feed in the best pastures, would roast a few head to eat during the trip. The meat, carried on the back of mules or horses, ended up getting salted by the animal's sweat and would be prepared in the evening at the rest stop.

With the emergence of the large cattle ranches, the so-called *estâncias*, the tradition was maintained by the cowboys who drove the cattle. These men, who journeyed across the pampas, with the minuano[2] blowing in their ears, dug deep trenches so that the hot coals would remain protected from the wind and, on wooden skewers, they would prepare the meat with the same coarse salt that they brought along to feed the cattle. The skewers stuck in the ground vertically, in a position opposite to the wind, enabled the meat to be grilled slowly by the heat blown from the coals. Without removing the meat from the skewer, the cowboys would serve themselves, cutting slices with a knife, while they kept up the conversation. And over the same fire, they would place a tripod on which they prepared the *arroz de carreteiro* (rice with jerked beef) and warmed the water for the *chimarrão* or mate tea.

But the origin of the so-called *espeto corrido* (literally translated as *running skewer)*, in which skewers with pieces of varied meat are served tableside in rotation (*rodízio*, in Portuguese) is a polemic subject with quite distinct versions. The one most disseminated says that the *"corrido"* began in an establishment on the edge of the BR116 highway, possibly at Jacupiranga, the current municipality of Registro, on the border between the States of Paraná and São Paulo. The story alleges that the establishment's owner, the gaucho of Italian origin Albino Ongaratto, seeing the restaurant full and the *churrascaria* crowded, supposedly suggested to the waiters that instead of serving one skewer for each table, they were to bring it to every table in turn. And what had merely been

a bright idea to deal with the crowd situation had become a great success, told and retold by the truckers across many highways, ending up being adopted by all the large *churrascarias*.

Another version says that the birthplace of the *espeto corrido* is the municipality of Taquara, in Rio Grande do Sul, at the Churrascaria Cruzeiro, owned by Toninho Machado who, in 1946, adopted the skewer with varied meats as a measure to avoid waste.

There are also those who defend the idea that the famous *espeto* was invented in the gaucho municipality of Sapiranga, in the 1950s, at the Churrascaria Mathias. In addition, there are those who defend the version that the *rodízio* was actually invented by a fumbling waiter who, in the midst of the intensive movement at the *churrascaria*

where he worked, confused the orders, bringing the dishes to the wrong tables. To resolve the confusion, the manager decided that all the dishes that were being ordered were to be served at all the tables.

The fact is that the influence of the Italian immigrants had already added to the traditional beef *churrasco* also the meats of lamb, pork and fowl. Furthermore, regardless of where it was invented, done either way, the *rodízio* system was and continues to be an enormous success.

---

[1] The Serra Gaúcha, or Gaucho Highlands, are situated in the State of Rio Grande do Sul, at the border with Uruguay, characterized by the presence of undergrowth and sparse small bushes. The name *pampa* is of quéchua origin and means "flat region."
[2] A cold wind typical of Rio Grande do Sul and the southern region of the State of Santa Catarina.

There wasn't much money but there was energy to spare by the young businessmen who opened the first branch of their Fogo de Chão in the Cavalhada suburb of Porto Alegre

the restaurant itself. The result was that as the months went by the salaries of both of them were left practically untouched and thus they built up the capital required to leverage their project to become businessmen.

Going back to the roots: birth of the Fogo de Chão in Porto Alegre

Snack bar? Minimarket? Restaurant? The important thing was to remain independent while operating a quality establishment. It had to be good. And return a profit, of course. At the same time, they longed for home and the two intended to return to Rio Grande do Sul and structure their business there. It fell to Arri, already 18 years old to travel to Porto Alegre to explore the opportunities.

One of his sisters lived in the city at this time and introduced him to a real-estate broker who took him directly to the site. It was called Fogo de Chão and had existed since 1979, in the Cavalhada district, about 1,000 meters distant from the Guaíba River. The restaurant opened only three days a week, in the evening, offering à la carte service, and the owners were thinking of disposing of the business. It was agreed that on the first sign that they would really sell, Arri would be told. And that was how it went.

Two months later the telephone rang. Jair, who was on vacation in Porto Alegre, would close the deal. All that was lacking was the money. No matter how hard they had saved they would be unable on their own to gather the entire purchase amount. It was then that the brothers Jorge and Aleixo Ongaratto, known by Arri from their job in Rio, were invited to become partners in the deal. All of them born in the same region, raised under the same values, two pairs of young and ambitious brothers.

Jair and Aleixo became acquainted on the occasion of the company's formal incorporation. The year was 1981, and the two closed the deal. Thus was born the new company that maintained the name of Fogo de Chão, but with a new spirit,

Features of the gaucho culture, present at the branches of the Fogo de Chão chain since its beginning. At the restaurant inaugurated in 1979, in Porto Alegre, the *churrasco* was served on a coarse table, in a shed covered with Santa Fé Grass. Left: in typical dress, the gauchos Jair and Arri Coser enjoy a mate tea infusion by the fireside, celebrating their first large venture

valuing the Brazilian roots, and the *churrasco* as the typical food of the South. Mr. Ângelo contributed in a fundamental manner to this big step taken by the sons. Together, Arri and Jair owned roughly 50% of the company's stock. The rest their father provided by means of the money saved by him in the course of his 50 years. But regardless of his belief in his sons' potential, he could surely not imagine the great success eventually achieved by Fogo de Chão.

The beginning was tough. One of the advantages enjoyed by the owners was their youth and willingness to face the work that included opening the restaurant, buying, preparing, selling and closing, that is, everything. There were left 2 or 3 hours for an almost re-storing sleep. Also an advantage, and a basic one, was the fact that they had a clear idea of their goals and values: a business of referential quality, differentiated and profitable. It proved to be an intensive learning curve, with daily mistakes and successes. But the investment had to become successful.

Four waiters were part of the team which already worked at the new restaurant under the old management, all of them a good deal older than the young men who had arrived to become their bosses. Experienced and dedicated, they taught a lot to the new owners and remained there for a long while, facing the challenge of gradually adapting the service offered by the former owners to the new rotating skewer service.

The grassroots music animated the nights at Fogo de Chão. In charge of production: Arri Coser

Valuing their roots, the owners of Fogo de Chão invested in the nativist movement, which was very strong at the time, and by opening the house to regional artists made their restaurant located in the Cavalhada suburb a destination to those who enjoyed good gaucho music

There was a clientele accustomed to a restaurant that opened from Thursdays through Saturdays offering à la carte service. It was necessary to attract new customers, creating a marketing strategy without expenses, as there was no money to spend. It was time to recover the investment and begin to earn money.

The place had style. Fogo de Chão occupied a shed roofed with Santa Fé grass, walls covered in leather and rustic furniture, forming a typically gaucho ambiance. There was a strong nativist movement at the time and the partners decided to wager on artists who were committed to redeeming and valuing the local culture. Fogo de Chão went on to promote shows Mondays, Tuesdays and Wednesdays. But since the restaurant was 12 km distant from the city's downtown area, this strategy required an enticing advertising campaign. Thank Heaven for the telephone! Arri took charge of calling all the names in an extensive list, inviting them to attend the shows. And things were proving successful, thanks to a mixture of culture and experience that the four partners had acquired working in Rio and São Paulo. The service was steadily improving, and the restaurant got more crowded day by day, while any debts were being eliminated.

The first Fogo de Chão became a point of reference not only to the dwellers in the city but especially to those who visited it. Artists, politicians, businessmen, athletes, journalists, arriving from all over Brazil, enjoyed the delicious *churrasco* competently served. Many became friends of the house and encouraged the partners to set their sights on higher ventures, heading for São Paulo, Brazil's financial capital.

The musician and composer César Camargo Mariano was one of these "advisors." Another strong encouragement was given by the journalist of the São Paulo capital, specialized in gastronomy, Silvio Lancelotti who, impressed by the quality of the service and by the products offered, on returning home wrote an article about the *churrascaria* in Porto Alegre and suggested to the owners that they seek him out in São Paulo. Whether it was a coincidence or not, 15 months after this episode had occurred, a good opportunity arose in São Paulo and the owners of Fogo de Chão took a decisive step in the history of their business.

Homebaked bread by Mrs. Leontina

On recalling the time in which the youngest son left his parent's home to face life away from home, Mrs. Leontina feels moved. She remembers how she greatly missed Arri when it became afternoon snack time, when he stuffed himself with homemade bread spread with chimia (jam) prepared by her with loving care.

Ingredients for 3 loaves:
- 2 eggs
- 1 tablespoon of instant dry yeast
- Approximately 600 g of wheat flour
- 1 dessert spoon salt
- 1 dessert spoon sugar
- Approximately 100 ml of filtered water
- Corn husks or oil to smear the loaf pans

Preparation:
- Mix the eggs and yeast, add the salt and sugar, the flour and water until the dough acquires a light consistency, although without being "liquid."
- Knead the dough until it becomes homogenous and smooth, let it stand for 1 hour.
- Place dough in pans and them place in the oven at a temperature of 250° for 40 minutes.

FOGO
DE
CHÃO

CHURRASCARIA
BRAZILIAN STEAKHOUSE

FOGO
DE
CHÃO

CHURRASCARIA
Brazilian Steakhouse

Chapter 2

The opportunity to install a new restaurant in São Paulo, within an area of 800 square meters on the Moreira Guimarães Avenue, was very appealing to the gauchos. Until then, the site had housed a boat dealership. The bet made by the new owners took into account the immense number of cars that drove by every day and the proximity of the Congonhas Airport. It was a large step but the young entrepreneurs took on the challenge. They needed a good attorney and José Amorim Linhares

Fogo de Chão
embraces Brazil

was referred to them to provide advice regarding the property's rental process and the company's installation. It so happened that on his first visit to the office situated in the Ipiranga suburb, just as he arrived, Jair ran into the owner of the property that they intended to rent.

The Moema branch, on Avenida Moreira Guimarães, close to the Congonhas Airport

On March 6, 1986, Fogo de Chão inaugurated its first branch in São Paulo, bringing the authentic gaucho *churrasco* to the city

By sheer coincidence, the tenant was a client of that same attorney and the same accountant. Suspicious, the young man avoided any further contact. But time and renewed recommendations brought him back to the office of Linhares, who advised them in the structuring of the business and closely followed its evolution.

The attorney was a witness to the the work schedule of the partners who worked a daily shift which began at 7:00 in the morning, with the restaurant's opening, and ended at its close as late as 2:00 the

The first Fogo de Chão brochure left no room for doubt: "a piece of Rio Grande do Sul had been implanted into the São Paulo capital"

next morning. The four partners handled everything, ranging from the management to the skewers of meat served tableside. Maintaining the style of the restaurant in Porto Alegre, the furniture was rustic, there were no tablecloths, and the ambiance was gaucho-like. And the restaurant was a success, ever since its inauguration on March 6, 1986. Fogo de Chão began in São Paulo, already growing. Allied with the bold temperament, keen business acumen and the pair of brothers' fortunate association, the owners of Fogo de Chão were also very lucky.

Activity at each Fogo de Chão branch begins early every day, in order to offer the customer perfect service and a product of unequalled quality

Work, work, work.
Always and well

It is 8:00 a.m. when the headwaiter, the cleaning team and the first kitchen crew arrive at Fogo de Chão, in the Moema suburb of São Paulo. Now begins yet another day at this first restaurant of the chain to open in the capital of São Paulo, which today requires the work of 96 employees and receives roughly 600 customers a day. It is now time to begin organizing the kitchen, prepare meat cuts, skewers and seasoning at the *churrasqueira*, or rotisserie. These are the first steps in the "Fogo de Chão *ballet*," which is expressed in precise movements, standardization of processes, and excellence in the quality of products and services.

At 10:00 in the morning the fire has already been lit and activity inside the restaurant is intense. Outside, the city that never stops, is buzzing with cars, people and work! At the restaurant, situated on a strategic spot close to the country's busiest airport, the waiters will have served by the end of the day between 500 and 600 kilograms of meat: top sirloin, beef ribs, lamb, beef ancho, or rib eye, bottom sirloin, premium meat cuts. The lavish and varied salad buffet, prepared by seven kitchen staff, under the super-

It's 1:00 pm in the São Paulo capital and there is intense movement within the Fogo de Chão branch in Moema

vision of a nutritionist attentive to the quality of the products and procedures, begins to be assembled at 11:00 a.m.

Before noon the serving room is already prepared to receive the first customers, who often arrive well before this time, already on their way to the airport. When this happens, they are invited to wait for the restaurant's opening at the bar. The piped music is international and discreet. The profile of the restaurant's patrons, to a large extent made up of business men and women blends into the ambiance. The bar often functions as the location for a meeting or the closing of a contract.

The service that comprises 35 waiters, five *maîtres d'*, two service managers and 23 gaucho chefs, who carry out a sort of choreography across the dining room, begins once the customers have been brought to their tables. Small signals, precise looks, all is thought out and synchronized, so that the customers won't have to worry about anything and so that their desires and needs may be almost anticipated by the harmonious and efficient service. The same situation surely holds true in the other branches of the Fogo de Chão.

Dedication in the quest for quality

Even with all their determination and enterprising spirit, the four businessmen could hardly have imagined that the partnership begun in Porto Alegre, at the shed covered by Santa Fé grass that contained 120 seats, would reach such a size,

Gaucho, with great pride

Every September 20, when Gaucho Day is celebrated, it is party time at the Fogo de Chão branches in Brazil. Recalling the Farroupilha Revolution, begun in 1835, in the course of which the province of São Pedro do Rio Grande do Sul was proclaimed the Republic of Rio Grande, it is traditional to celebrate the date with cultural expressions that bring to mind gaucho values. At Fogo de Chão, the so-called Farroupilha Festival begins with an activity of integration among the employees of all the branches in Brazil, sponsored by the company's human resources division.

The idea was to promote a space for the exchange of knowledge and for collective building, based on the gaucho roots, common to the great majority of the team's members. The move was so successful that today it is part of the branch's yearly calendar. Transcending the limits of the company itself, the Farroupilha Festival ended up also involving the employees' family members in a grand event that comprises music, dancing, poetry, typical dishes and other cultural expressions. Preparing for the event requires great dedication from the artists, in regard both to the making of the typical dress and to rehearsals and production. The event became so popular that in subsequent years the participants' true talents have emerged.

The Farroupilha Revolution, or War of the Tatters (*Guerra dos Farrapos*), was the result of the people's dissatisfaction with the imperial government. Which imposed high taxes on the local production and lasted for 10 years, and at that time ended on the signing of a peace agreement. On this occasion, the Rio Grande Republic was dissolved and today is a part of the State of Rio Grande do Sul, being symbolically represented on the state's flag, perpetuating among the descendants of these lands their fighting tradition.

This respect for the regional history and culture is embedded in the roots of Fogo de Chão, which brings with it the gaucho values wherever it goes, by means of its branches.

From the authentic fire on the ground exhibited in the

wall showcase of each establishment to the costume of the employees in the dining room, not to mention their hospitality and courtesy, everything brings to mind the gaucho culture. But who, after all, is the gaucho? In the beginning, when the territory of the current Rio Grande do Sul was still wild, and the cattle that had escaped from the first Spanish settlements in the region ran about loose and multiplied, a gaucho was the Indian native, the Spaniard, the Portuguese, the *mestizo*, who lived freely roaming the world, without a boss or fixed abode, capturing cattle. This free man, in daily contact with the field and nature's stormy weather, developed a number of skills and peculiar customs, which facilitated his work, protected him from adversities and promoted a neighborly coexistence with those whom he met in the immensity of the countryside: the circle of men talking and drinking *chimarrão* (mate tea), dancing and musical rhythms, and the *fogo de chão* (fire on the ground or camp fire) *churrasco*.

With the advent of the cattle ranches, the gaucho went on to work within this structure, becoming the cowboy of the *estâncias* (ranches). The strength of this culture and the recognition of these men's fighting spirit, proven in the course of time, ended up making people employ the expression gaucho to designate the people born in Rio Grande do Sul.

The uniform of those who work in the Fogo de Chão dining rooms brings back to life the typical clothes of the gaucho: the *bombachas*, or baggy pants, that came to Brazil with the Turks and are held up at the waist by the *guaiaca*, a broad belt with pockets, made of leather, which in the countryside is used to carry money, tobacco, small objects and weapons. High top boots complement the costume, which includes a silken scarf knotted at the neck. Also part of the *pilcha*[1] (costume) are the poncho[2] and the hat.

[1] Name given to the complete gaucho costume.
[2] A sort of cloak made of wool, which can be used as a blanket for sleeping.

MELHORES PARTES PARA O CHURRASCO
BEST PARTS FOR BARBECUE

1 - Rabo / Ox Tail
2 - Lagarto / Eye of The Round
3 - Coxão Duro ou Chã de Fora / Outside Round
4 - Coxão Mole ou Chã de Dentro / Top Inside
5 - Músculo / Muscle - Shank
6 - Patinho / KnucKle
7 - *Picanha / Rumpsteak*
8 - *Alcatra / Top Sirloin*
9 - *Contra Filé Argentino (Noix) / Sirloin*
10 - *Filé Mignon / Tenderloin*
11 - Aba de Filé / Skirt of Tenderloin Beef
12 - *Fraldinha / Botton Sirloin*
13 - *Ponta de Agulha / Short Ribs*
14 - Capa de Filé / Prime Rib
15 - Acém / Chuck
16 - Braço, Pá ou Paleta / Shoulder
17 - Peito / Breast
18 - Pescoço / Neck
19 - Filé de Costela / Strip Loin
20 - *Maminha de Alcatra / Trip-Tip*
21 - *Cupim / Hump*

Brasil

Santo Amaro - SP
(11) 5524-0500

Moema - SP
(11) 5056-1795

Vila Olimpia - SP
(11) 5505-0791

Belo Horizonte - MG
(31) 3227-2730

FOGO DE CHÃO ®
CHURRASCARIA
DESDE 1979

USA

Dallas - TX
(972)503-7300

Chicago - IL
(312)932-9330

Houston - TX
(713)978-6500

Beverly Hills - CA
(310)289-7755

Atlanta - GA
(404)266-9988

Washington - DC
(202)347-4668

http://www.fogodechao.com.br

Originality is an important part of the Fogo de Chão philosophy. Everything is carried out according to the brand's quality and efficiency standard, ranging from the cuts of meat to the decor details at each location

30 years later. That their Fogo de Chão was to establish a new level in terms of a gaucho-style steakhouse, transforming into a gastronomic experience what used to be perceived as an ordinary meal taken at a roadside diner while traveling, to imagine that their brand, full of tradition, would turn into a synonym of excellence recognized in Brazil and worldwide, that would lead the gaucho regional cuisine to represent Brazil abroad, or is it possible that they already envisaged this entire eventual outcome?

To begin with, the partners opted for the system of working in different areas of the company, so that each one would obtain an understanding of the entire business. Thus, each week one of them would take over a different area, working the rotisserie, purchasing the meats, customer service, contacts with the artists who performed at the restaurant, management, in short, being in charge of everything that concerned the good operation of the business according to the standard that Fogo de Chão had aimed at since the beginning. Guided by intuition, they hit on the right method. The system of working in alternate areas proved to be a schooling for each one of them and consolidated the partnership.

During that time of taking large steps nothing could go wrong. Or nearly nothing. This required criteria that began with the careful selection of the suppliers. It was fundamental to work with people that they could really trust, because more than just suppliers they sought partners that aimed at achieving excellence in the business. This was the profile of Aldo Carboni, another native of the Serra Gaúcha who had also exchanged the farm for the city.

Aldo relates that he always knew that the quartet would go far,

FOGO DE CHÃO
O MAIOR ESPETÁCULO DA CARNE

Vinte e cinco anos depois da primeira casa – um chalé de capim em Porto Alegre – a churrascaria brasileira que serve um milhão de rodízios por ano para os americanos está abrindo sua quinta filial nos Estados Unidos. E em Beverly Hills, chão de estrelas

Por Celso A...

Da primeira Fogo de Chão c...
Unidos (na foto, a filial de Chic...

A Fo-go dè...
am o n...
lial ho...
point co...
caria cria...
de irmãos...
quatro *Fo-go dèe Shown* am...
serviram um milhão de fregu...
as contas. Ali, em 2004, fora...
ma sobrar nos pratos um mis...

16

CHURRASCO
CHURRASCARIAS

GANHE
uma churrasqueira

ARQUITETURA
OS CUIDADOS NA REFORMA
DAS CHURRASCARIAS

NUTRIÇÃO
OS BENEFÍCIOS DA
CARNE BOVINA

CACHAÇA
SUGESTÕES PARA
MONTAR UMA CARTA

Arri Coser
SUCESSO BRASILEIRO
NOS ESTADOS UNIDOS

CONSUMO

Inauguração de mais uma rede nacional na cidade acirra a
concorrência pelo mercado de rodízio de alto padrão em BH

Churrasco de luxo
conquista capital

ZULMIRA FURBINO

O avanço das churrascarias de alto padrão não esn... queima de rodízio reforçou um novo hábito do consumidor de Belo Horizonte. Até o fim de 2002, apenas a Adega do Sul, fundada há 26 anos, atuava nesse segmento. De lá para cá, a capital mineira ganhou mais quatro casas e o lance mais ousado na disputa...

ao ano e terceira maior da mar... no país, superada apenas pela d... Aterro do Flamengo, no Rio, e a d... Brasília. Só em Belo Horizonte, sã... servidos 17 mil a 20 mil rodízi... por mês. "Quando resolvem... abrir a casa, muita...

Economia e Negócios

A CARNE
É FORTE

A Fogo de Chão chegou depois aos Estados Unidos, em 1997, mas teve uma expansão mais rápida. Há no...

o dobro dos clientes brasileiros. "O que garantiu nosso sucesso aqui nos Estados Unidos foi a previsibilidade da economia americana", diz Arri Coser.

... legislação trabalhista nos Estados ... flexível do que a brasilei...

サンパウロで最も選びぬかれた
味のシュラスカリア。クッピン、
ピッカーニャなどの微妙な味わ
いをお楽しみください。

A MELHOR CARNE/RODÍZIO

FOGO DE CHÃO - Sempre vestidos com bombachas gaúchas, os afáveis e bem treinados garçons passam entre as mesas e oferecem a picanha sumarenta, a substanciosa fraldinha, o bife ancho premium extramacio, o cordeirinho fabuloso... Esses e outros cortes são o patrimônio do Fogo de Chão, reconhecido pela quarta vez como o melhor rodízio. Para abrir ou acompanhar a refeição, o belo bufê limita-se a saladas e itens como azeites importados até do Líbano. Nada de frutos do mar nem pratos japoneses, comuns na maioria dos congêneres. Aqui, a estrela é tão-somente a carne. Inaugurada na capital gaúcha em 1979, a casa veio para São Paulo sete anos depois com seu espeto corrido, como é chamado o rodízio nos pampas. De lá para cá, multiplicou-se por três endereços. Nem o preço de R$ 59,00, superior ao de todos os demais da categoria, refreia o clientão. O sucesso é tamanho que os proprietários têm planos de expansão, com a abertura de uma unidade em Santana no próximo ano. **Avenida Santo Amaro, 6824,** Santo Amaro, ☎ 5524-0500 (280 lugares); **Avenida Moreira Guimarães, 964,** Moema, ☎ 5056-1795 (320 lugares); **Avenida dos Bandeirantes, 538,** Brooklin, ☎ 5505-0791 (320 lugares). 12h/16h e 18h/0h (sáb. sem intervalo; dom. sem intervalo até 22h30). Cc.: todos. Cd.: M, R e V. Estac. c/manobr. ☺ ⌂ ♫ — www.fogodechao.com.br. Aberto em 1986. $$$$

EMPREENDEDORES

Cortes
sofisticados
também
nas carnes

know-how brasileiro
conquista e cresce no
mercado internacional

...nsylvania Avenue, Was...
...gton D.C. A avenida sim...
...do poder na capital
...ricana — a Casa Branca...
1600 — abriga, desde o...
de dezembro, o brasi...
...Chão. É a nova casa...
mãos Coser abrem...
...e que, somadas...
sas no Brasil, lhes...
...amento, no ano...
...hões, vendendo...
unhado de bu...
por pessoa no...
... do Tio Sam,...
...batizado de...

abre, na segunda quinzena de janeiro, uma churrascaria em Madri, com o nome de Juan Ramos Jimenez, ao lado do estádio do Real Madri. Nossa for... meros tipos de carne e incomparável... bufês (mesmo sendo o churrasco he... rança comum de todo os gaúchos se... jam brasileiros, argentinos ou uru... guaios) conquista o mundo. Acostuma... dos com as churrascarias, nós não per... cebemos as mudanças que as transfor... maram em big business no universo da... alimentação e do turismo.

O chef francês Joel Robuchon, elei... to o melhor chef do século XX pelo guia Gault-Millau, lançou, certa vez, em conversa com jornalista brasilei... ros em São Paulo, com esteve a co... vite do chef Laurent Suadeau, uma idéia inusitada. Ele se pergunta se o churrasco não poderia ser a gran... de contribuição brasileira à gastrono...

GASTRONOMIA

por Silvio Lancellotti
Jornalista, chef de cozinha e escritor

Duas décadas de
Fogo de Chão em São Paulo

Americanos e turistas (inclusive brasileiros) aprovam o churrasco gaúcho do

Fogo de Chão, nos EUA

Foto: Gladsto...

Para quem viaja para os Estados Unidos, a dica é conhecer uma das churrascarias da Fogo de Chão em 6 diferentes cidades: Dallas, Houston, Chicago, Atlanta, Beverly Hills e Washington. Em quanto qualquer casa que escolher vai se sentir no Brasil e poderá saborear o serviço corrido de qualidade e conferir o serviço impecável que são marcas registradas da Fogo de Chão de São Paulo...

...drão de qualidade. Em janeiro de 2000, a cidade de Houston foi escolhida para abri-gar a segunda casa do grupo, seguida por Atlanta, em 2001 e Chicago, em 2002.

A quinta casa da Fogo de Chão em Beverly Hills, Los Angeles, Califórnia, com-pletou um ano de atividades em março de 2006, recebendo diariamente astros famo-sos, turistas e personalidades do mundo inteiro. A churrascaria oferece 100 lugares em ambientes com uma decoração moderna re...

...firma o sucesso que faz o espeto corrido gaúcho, que oferece cerca de quinze cor-tes, com cinco diferentes tipos de carne: a costela feita no fogo de chão, picanha, fral-dinha, bife ancho e cordeiro, estes, entre as mais consumidas nos Estados Unidos e também no Brasil.

"A matéria-prima provém de diferen-tes procedências - Uruguai, Argentina, Chile e Nova Zelândia ligar fornece e-x-celente cordeiro da casa). além do interior de São Paulo, Paraná e o Rio Grande do Sul - tudo cuidadosamente selecionado...

... Chicago - Estados Unidos

EXPORTAÇÃO

Entrevista

Arri Coser

Exemplo de sucesso no Brasil e nos EUA, Arri Coser, proprietário da rede de churrascarias Fogo de Chão, conta um pouco sobre sua trajetória e se prepara para mais um grande passo: a abertura da sexta casa americana. Segundo Arri, o segredo de tamanho prestígio está no aprimoramento regular da mão-de-obra e na busca constante pela satisfação do cliente.

Textos Rita Moraes
Fotos: Divulgação

Alta Gastronomia: Como
se iniciou no ramo da gastronomia...

Com restaurantes no
Texas e na Geórgia,
Fogo de Chão fatura
mais nos EUA do
que no Brasil

onvencida de que a globaliza-ção pode ser uma de mão du-pla, a churrascaria Fogo de Chão, tradicional casa de rodízio com três lojas no Brasil (duas em São Paulo e uma em Porto Alegre) chegou nos Estados Unidos há quatro anos. O sucesso tem sido tão grande que já está sendo preparada a abertura de um novo restaurante, o quarto, em breve, no Barbecue. Ela está programada para o próximo ano, em Chicago. Além de poder apreciar o churrasco à moda gaúcha, os americanos estilo descobrindo as delícias de acompanhamentos como feijão preto, arroz, vinagrete, pão de queijo na entrada e as mais variadas caipirinhas. O cardápio e a maneira de servir são idênticos aos das churrascarias do Brasil. De quebra, os clientes de lá estão aprendendo a pronunciar o nome da casa – 'fo-go dèe chão'...

A meta é abrir
uma loja por
ano no exterior
até 2006

O sucesso do
"Fo-go dèe Sıown"

1997, quando a Fogo de Chão che-gou a Dallas. A qualidade da carne da Texas e o grupo de três texanos pelos qual galardão tiveram peso considerável em escolha. Assim, a empresa resolveu percorrer caminhos inversos aos de nossas redes brasileiras – como a churrascaria carioca Porcão e Plataforma e o paulista Habib's – que preferiram estrear na Passada Unida nos Estados Unidos e provavelmente tam-bém na Europa, para atingir grandes clientelas imigra...

Dallas, com nove pessoas, controla o abastecimento e a administração das três lojas, além de planejar a expansão do grupo. "O sucesso tem sido tão grande que principiamos abrir uma loja a cada ano até 2005. E, até 2010, a meta é inaugurar duas por ano, nos Estados Unidos e provavelmente tam-bém na Europa, para onde daria o primeiro grande passo", confirma Coser.

Que restaurante?

Em 2001, as lojas nos Estados Unidos deverão faturar perto de US$ 35 milhões – quase quatro vezes mais o movimento agregado com as...

três churrascarias no Brasil. Cerca de 90% dos fregueses são americanos e os outros 10% latinos. O gasto médio por cliente aproxima-se de US$ 60. Cada casa serve em média 18 mil refeições por mês. "Recordo nos Es-tados Unidos" Até agora dão dez para outra", comenta Coser.

Destaque aqui, uma loja que ad-quiriu seu melhor no preço – dos 300 empregados conquistam e se benefi-ciam com serviços de advocacia e de benefícios. Recebem treinamento especial e ferreas cores de regalidade contínuo pela Fogo de Chão, antes de

... ao vivo ao cliente americano a mais típica fórmula gaúcha de assar carnes – logo à entrada das lojas, como no Brasil, o cliente depara com uma fogueira sobre piso de pedra. É de serviu-lo segundo o sistema de espeto corrido – denominação gaúcha para o popular rodízio (*continuous service*, em inglês). O bufê de saladas é tão farto quanto o dos restaurantes Fogo de Chão brasileiros.

Destaque na mídia

Mais a maior vantagem do sucesso advém da qualidade das carnes gaú-chas, graças em boa parte aos cortes especiais, aguçam a melhor técnica gaúcha. No total, são dezesseis varie-dades de cortes. "Treinamos nossos fornecedores no sentido de oferecer um churrasco praticamente idêntico ao que pode ser consumido em nossa casa no Brasil", afirma Coser. Em março deste ano, o *Houston Business Journal* creveu a Fogo de Chão, como a sexta melhor churrascaria...

Washington DC, sempre nos Estados Unidos. Um controle de qualidade rigorosíssimo faz com que, mesmo no exterior, ...na convivência com hábitos diversos, a Fogo de Chão fulgi... independentemente do clima e da geografia.

O empenho dos proprietários, e a eficiência das brigadas de grelha e de atendimento, excepcionalmente treina... acaba de lhes assegurar, de acordo com a revista *Veja São Pa...* pela quinta vez consecutiva, o laurel de "Melhor Carne/Rod... da cidade. Uma justa homenagem ao conjunto da obra e dos C... & Ongarotto, que não se limitam a privilegiar os seus corte... carne, excepcionais. No seu endereço mais novo, avenida... Bandeirantes, os *barmen* preparam os drinques corretos... mais exigentes. E, depois do mergulho no precioso bufê de...

ever since the time when the butcher's shop that he had opened in Porto Alegre supplied Fogo de Chão with meat. Also starting out on his journey, he recognized the potential of that couple of brothers, who were unafraid to work, and were always investing in the business' improvement: one day replacing the floor, another day the roof, putting in improved tables, better-looking cutlery. Without any managerial experience, with little resources and a lean team, they were guided by common sense and invested heavily in differentiation obtained by means of quality. To be a supplier of these businessmen with a veritable obsession for offering the best was almost a privilege. A privilege to be able to meet a growing demand and to be a partner in the improvement of the meat cuts,

and in the research and development of increasingly better products.

These were times of scarcity of products and, differently from what occurs today, when it is possible to acquire exactly those portions of the bull that the buyer wants to consume, the buying and selling operations were actually the so-called bundled product sales. That is, if the buyer was interested in beef ribs, he had to buy the entire forequarter and hindquarter. Aldo, who did the purchasing then, had to find buyers for the cuts that didn't interest the fellow operators of Fogo de Chão. Everything that was unsuited to the good *churrasco*, or Brazilian gaucho-style barbecue, served table-side by the restaurant, was offered, even at a lower price, to other customers, often located at a considerable distance away. But even so it was an advantage to the butcher to work with Fogo de Chão. These were fully trustworthy people, operating a proper company, which grew by linking its brand to excellence of quality and in addition went after increasingly better meats, raising also the standard of its product in the market.

This affinity of interests and market visions relative to its partners was to become a banner of Fogo de Chão which, based on the mindful search for the best of everything, has been challenging its suppliers to invest in the development of differentiated products and processes, relying on the brand's prestige.

Work, unity and respect: thus was Fogo de Chão built. Below, the brothers Diole, Jair and Arri Coser working together at the start of the Porto Alegre branch

Growing apace with the economic plans

In February 1986, the then President of the Republic, José Sarney, decreed the so-called Cruzado Plan. The hyperinflation of nearly 230% a year devoured wages; among the main measures of the package to restrain the inflationary escalation was the suspension of monetary correction and the substitution of the then current currency. Having its value divided by 1,000, the cruzeiro was replaced by the cruzado. Thus, 1,000 cruzeiros became worth one cruzado. A large impact was also caused by the freezing of prices for a one-year period.

In the midst of these intense upheavals, the gauchos of Fogo de Chão opened the doors in São Paulo charging reasonable prices, while the competition maintained its prices frozen. The restaurant's first six months of operation resulted in exceptional growth: everything that was available was sold. The company had sufficient breath to withstand the subsequent moment of general supply shortage in the country. Production was incapable of keeping up with the escalation of consumption, which compelled Fogo de Chão to purchase food articles in Argentina and Uruguay all the while maintaining quality, even in the course of this difficult period.

Whether it was a coincidence, luck or simply business acumen, in subsequent economic plans Fogo de Chão also benefited from excellent operations, always emerging strong from these moments of turbulence and investing in its own growth. In 1986, the partners carried out the first expansion of the branch at Moema, in São Paulo, by means of the acquisition of adjacent lots. In 1990, they incorporated an additional 400 meters to the restaurant that began with a capacity for 280 people and which since 2003 occupies an area of 2,000 meters, and is now capable of accommodating 400 people in its dining room.

Fogo de Chão established a unique *churrascaria* standard. No longer the roadside
diner, but rather a gastronomical destination

Dining room yarns

A heritage from the Guarani Indian people, the *chimarrão*, or mate tea, is the typical beverage of Rio Grande do Sul. It is prepared and served in a gourd, in which the yerba mate is placed and hot water is then poured on top of it. Always bitter, it is drunk by means of a metal straw[1]. The custom of drinking *chimarrão* is known as *matear*.

Somebody suggests: let's *matear*? And this is the best time to tell a few yarns sitting round the *chimarrão* circle following, of course, the entire ritual of the old tradition. The first gourd belongs to the *cevador*[2], then the round of drinking begins with the oldest participant present or with somebody that one wishes to please. For instance, a guest. When the gourd has emptied, it always returns to the hands of the *cevador* who then prepares the leaves and refills the gourd with hot water. And there is always room for one more participant. If someone says thank you to the *cevador* it means that he no longer wants to *matear*. But, even so, he may remain in the circle and tell tales.

[1] The *chimarrão* metal straw, called the *bomba*, has the shape of a metal straw, which at one end has what appears to be a closed spoon, but is full of small holes. This part of the straw remains in contact with the wet yerba mate and it is through this straw that the liquid rises while "filtered" by the straw.
[2] The person who prepares the *chimarrão*

He may recall stories such as the many tales that have already been experienced in the Fogo de Chão dining rooms.

And in regard to the Formula One, it is worth pointing out that Fogo de Chão is almost a unanimity among racing-car drivers who, as a rule, gather with their teams to celebrate their victories. Or not. And English is the language most often used on these occasions. Well then, once a driver called a waiter to ask for ice and with the usual efficiency of the restaurant's service, the employee brought to the table a dish of rice. "Ice" said one, "rice" understood the other, no one was able to understand what was happening until the service manager came to save the customer, who was then able to drink his iced juice. As regards the waiter: it was suggested that he reinforce his English lessons!

But it isn't only the English language that has caused an employee to stumble. Once, a client passed along the buffet and asked the waiter where the *toillete* was, to which the waiter replied: "No, sir. We have no spaghetti in the buffet." But this was yet one more customer saved by the restaurant's efficient teamwork: "This way, sir," concluded an employee who just happened to be passing by as the problem occurred.

And if situations of this sort happened in Brazil it was to be expected that they would occur even more frequently on the

arrival of Fogo de Chão in the United States. Regardless of how much the team was prepared for change, only the day-to-day experience could put the employees to the test and many were the misunderstandings in the dining room until the language had been mastered.

The introduction of the differentiated service also caused curious reactions. The regional manager of Fogo de Chão in Chicago, Minneapolis and Indianapolis, Sidiclei de Martini, remembers the day in which a state governor visited the branch in Chicago. It was his first time at the *churrascaria* and, captivated by the experience, he asked to be allowed to take home one of the cards that are placed on the table and serve to signal the waiter whether or not the customer wants to be served: green on one side, red on the other. He explained that he would like to take the card with him because he had a meeting with people who were going to ask him for money and he would then use the card to signal green in case of his approval and red if he disapproved. And he left directly for the office, actually taking the card along.

An unforgettable episode was experienced by the current director of operations of Fogo de Chão in Brazil, Jandir Dalberto, during his initial stint at the company. Born in Paraná, a descendant of Italian immigrants, the boy Jandir

was called on to drink *chimarrão*, always prepared by his mother. Differently from what was the custom in the home of a gaucho, Jandir was never interested in learning to prepare the *chimarrão*. He drank the beverage but did not prepare it and when he began work at Fogo de Chão in São Paulo, didn't worry about this at all. He couldn't possibly imagine that this lack of knowledge would put him in trouble on the occasion of a live broadcast of a series of TV programs on cooking, with recipes, interviews and curiosities, which employed Fogo de Chão as the scenario. Jandir underwent training, a stage better known as the "observation period." And on the day in which one of the themes of the program would be the chimarrão, or Mate tea, Mr. Arri spoke to him: "Jandir, go wash your face and comb your hair, the program will begin within five minutes and you will explain how the Mate is prepared. Hurry!" The young man's despair nearly paralyzed him, in couldn't possibly allow himself to disappoint the boss. He felt badly, unprepared, but had to face the challenge. When an employee of the restaurant delivered the gourd to him, Jandir gave vent to his feelings: "Young woman, I've never prepared a *chimarrão*. How does one do it? I've always watched my mother doing it, but I myself don't know how." And his coworker, showing solidarity, explained: "Stay cool. Place the tea here, shake the gourd three times, and then..." And the TV program began, with no delay at all. Jandir recalls that he hardly felt his feet within the boots, he was that nervous, but full of boldness he not only prepared his first *chimarrão* while live on TV, and in color, but in addition gave an explanation on the origin of the beverage. He was 21 years old at the time.

But it isn't only the people of the south of Brazil who appreciate *chimarrão*. All the Orientals who are frequent visitors at Fogo de Chão end up becoming charmed by the beverage and the habit of *matear*. Even Prince Naruhito, of Japan, in a visit to Brazil drank mate at Fogo de Chão.

And we will continue to *matear* and tell yarns!

The branch at Santo Amaro

In 1987, Fogo de Chão had been installed in Santo Amaro, a district of the São Paulo capital characterized by a strong concentration of German immigrants and their descendants, besides Americans and other European people. Within an extensive territory, the district gathers an important business complex and a residential area with roughly 3 million dwellers, most of which belong to the A and B income classes.

Opening a new branch was not a priority of the partners, but a proposal was made to take over the business which wasn't doing so well under the former owner and the partners decided to purchase the location. There was a problem: they had no guarantor. The solution, although seemingly improbable, was easy. The property's seller assumed the role of guarantor of the transaction, closed so as to last for a long term, and the restaurant underwent an extensive restoration and was inaugurated on June 18.

Opening in 1987, the Moema branch was the first to introduce air conditioning and refrigerated buffet, among other innovations

The refrigerated buffet and other novelties were also implemented at the Moema unit. Fogo de Chão now repositioned the *churrasco* concept in the market. Far different from the smoky restaurant, in which it was impossible to enjoy a meal without leaving the premises smelling of meat, the Fogo de Chão steakhouse was a glamorous restaurant, truly a space offering top-level gastronomy.

The trips made abroad went on to become part of the strategy of the company's updating and improvement: details concerning the service, the products, everything was the object of research and evolution. But, even so, the work wasn't any lighter. The partners continued to carry out alternate shifts at the branches, performing various functions. This system of working extended over roughly seven years and produced excellent results.

Attentive to everything, the partners realized that the presence of foreigners at the branches might be a trump. That is, to have employees born in the country's south, the descendants of Italians and Germans, might be an excellent idea, even if they weren't the best in the language of their forebears. And thus it was done. Once an Italian customer had been identified, a waiter was designated to serve the customer, surprising him by speaking his language. The same

held true for the German customer. And in the same manner the customer who spoke English was preferably served by waiters who had worked in the aviation industry and spoke a bit of English. It was like an army committed to winning over the market, offering the customers a differentiated service.

Close to the Interlagos Racing Track, the Santo Amaro branch became a point of reference to the Formula One drivers and their teams, which frequently celebrated their victories by savoring a gaucho-style *churrasco*. No one would have imagined that the strategy to implement this so efficient and personalized service had been decided on right there in the dining room or the kitchen. To begin with there was no office available at the branch and, when it was built, it was small and offered no air conditioning, making it impossible to remain in it for a long while. So much so that the partners used to say that this had been done on purpose in order that they would always be together with those that really interested them: the customers.

Being a customer of Fogo de Chão

Possibly because he or she feels valued and understands that Fogo de Chão is, and wants to continue always being a token of quality, the frequent customer of Fogo de Chão ends up creating bonds of a true partnership, almost as if they were family. At least that is what one perceives in the contacts with numerous customers historically faithful to Fogo de Chão, such as the woman who frequented the Santo Amaro branch, who declares: "I haven't had a good week unless I visit Fogo de Chão at least once." That is how Mrs. Taís sums up her relations with the restaurant that she has frequented ever since its inauguration. She and her husband Ralf visit Fogo de Chão regularly on Saturdays. A routine that is set aside only when an engagement that cannot be turned down crops up on a Saturday evening and they are then compelled to visit Fogo de Chão on the Friday. The branch's team is already acquainted with their habits and preferences and welcomes them as good friends of long standing: ten years!

Another instance of passionate feeling for Fogo de Chão is that of the Zaidan family. One could say that the couple Marcelo and Ana Maria and their children Felipe and Eduardo "punch their time card" at Fogo de Chão; the boys, ever since they were born, and the couple a good while before the boys were born. They affectionately relate that in the past 20 years they have frequented Fogo de Chão practically every week, having several good stories to tell: "When they were small, our children slept in chairs placed together by the waiters, thus improvising a cradle, while we enjoyed our lunch. After they took their first steps, they were tied to the baby high chair with the scarf that is typical of the gaucho attire. Elsewhere, we usually had to beg our sons to eat but at Fogo de Chão they were always hearty eaters, which encouraged us to continue frequenting the restaurant."

Marcelo and Ana Maria recall their apprehension when they learned that some of their dear friends, who had served them for years and years, might leave Brazil to work in the United States, to where Fogo de Chão was expanding. Apprehension accompanied by happiness because of the deserved promotion and opportunity given to such competent and dear people. Their apprehension was in relation to the future service to be offered: would it continue to be impeccable? But each waiter who left gave precise instructions about how the meat was to be prepared, cut and served to the Zaidan family, in such a manner that the service would always remain perfect. On a trip to the United States, the couple didn't miss the opportunity to get acquainted with the branches in Chicago, Washington and Philadelphia, meeting anew old friends who had served them for so many years.

The businessman Marcelo Zaidan, admittedly a gourmet, has already visited more than 60 countries, always seeking the best dishes available in each local cuisine. "I've visited the Michelin-star restaurants, but nowhere in the world did I find all the qualities offered at Fogo de Chão. Sometimes, for fun, when a customer dropped a cup on the floor, my son would immediately start his stopwatch. It never took more than 15 seconds for the busboy to appear and speedily pick up the shards."

In the 1990s, it was already apparent that the business would grow. Fogo de Chão invested in marketing and in the training of professionals suited for the structure that became increasingly professionalized

The 1990s: professionalizing the structure

It was certainly a lot of work, from the kitchen to the dining room, back to the cash register, then to the administration, and then again to purchasing and paying, then opening and closing… Even thought the partners were young, full of energy and good intentions, they thought that it was necessary to seek allies. On the occasion of the inauguration of the branches at Moema and Santo Amaro, the partners invited people of their close acquaintance, cousins and friends, to become part of the company.

To begin with, the family members left and professionals took over the managerial functions. Only in 1993 did the partners establish the functions of a *maître d'* and service manager, who today work together with the branch's general manager, supervised by the regional manager. This entire team works under the coordination of the operational director, just below the owners.

Playing on the Fogo de Chão team

"**A** unique opportunity." This is how most of the Fogo de Chão employees refer to their participation in the company. The journeys of many of those who today hold a managerial position in the restaurant chain, in both Brazil and the United States, run parallel to the very history of the Coser brothers: members of numerous gaucho families, descendants of immigrants installed in the country's south, bold youths who left the countryside to earn their living in the large city. On recalling the development of their careers, they unanimously affirm that Fogo de Chão accords great value to its human capital and knows how to ally standardization with diversity, and discipline with each employee's personal way of doing things.

Today the *maître d'* at Fogo de Chão in Moema, Luis da Silveira was born in 1994 in the interior of Erexim, a municipality of Rio Grande do Sul, whence he left for São Paulo to work at a *churrascaria* as kitchen assistant. Among his colleagues who worked in the restaurant field, he heard comments to the effect that Fogo de Chão was the best place to work: excellent salary, an opportunity to study English and to grow professionally. Proof of this was that a friend of his who worked at the company was going to the United States at the time. At the end of 1999, Luis began working at Fogo de Chão in Santo Amaro, in São Paulo, where he began as a cleaner. He recalls that in the morning shift he cleaned the entire dining room, from 11:00 in the morning to 3:00 in the afternoon, took care of the buffet and later would clean the dining room again readying it for the evening shift. Luis himself says that "I was a young *piá*[1], without any discernment and ended up leaving the company, but was given an opportunity to return and jumped at it. I was promoted to waiter. I've had room to grow and have been a *maître d'* since 2003."

It was also due to the good reputation of Fogo de Chão among the *churrascaria* staffs that Jandir Dalberto became interested in seeking a job at the company. On vacation from the steakhouse at which he worked, in Rio de Janeiro,

Jandir was traveling to visit his family in the south. At a bus stop in São Paulo, he met a young man who worked at Fogo de Chão. They sat together and in the course of the journey Jandir was amazed with his companion's story about his job and the manner in which he was recognized and valued. That was enough to make him call Fogo de Chão on their arrival at the border between the states of Paraná and Santa Catarina, telling his story and asking for a job. The manager at that time was receptive, and wanted him to begin work right away. The result of their talk over the telephone was that the visit to the family lasted only two days. Jandir returned to Rio, resigned from his job, went to São Paulo and started working as a waiter at the Santo Amaro Fogo de Chão branch in June 1990. Within 14 months he was promoted to manager and was directly responsible for the training of many of the employees who work at the restaurant today, in both Brazil and the United States. Later, Jandir was invited to take over the position of director of operations in Brazil, a function that he still exercises with immense satisfaction.

Stories of professional valuation and growth within the company are common. Thus it was with the great majority of those who today hold positions such as that of general manager, at each one of the branches, and other strategic positions in the business' administration. The Santa Catarina native Adriana Michel, responsible for the financial department of the chain in Brazil, is proud of having begun work at the company washing dishes and of having reached her current position on the strength of her personal merit and owing to the sensibility of the owners who perceived the value of their human resources.

The regional manager of Fogo de Chão in Baltimore and Washington, in the United States, Jean Boschetti, began working in the pantry of the Santo Amaro branch in São Paulo, in 1997, the same year in which Alda Boiani arrived in the United States as a member of the team of nine persons that was to work at the Dallas branch. Born and raised in the Serra Gaúcha, Alda began working at the cash register of one of the São Paulo branches and is today a member of the administrative division of Fogo de Chão in the United States, handling purchasing and contracts.

All those who were members of the team that left Brazil, called on to implement an arm of the business abroad, facing the challenge of becoming foreigners, perceived there an opportunity for growth, even though far from the family, friends, and the homeland... Except for the visual design of the branch at which they were to work, wearing the same uniform, serving with the same elegance and discipline, everything else would be different: the streets, the habits, the lodging and, worse, the language. These were difficult times, of adaptation, but which today are recalled with considerable good humor by those who persevered and overcame the challenge of planting the bases for the development of Fogo de Chão in the United States.

Elmir Bernardon belongs to this team. The general manager of the Atlanta branch, he began as a waiter and says that to begin with all the colleagues had to act as brothers to each other since one depended on the other to deal with the most ordinary things. Even to open a bank account it was necessary to join individual efforts to understand the language and make oneself understood. Together, they managed. Together, they celebrated Christmas and the New Year. Together they worked every day and lived in the same condominium. That constitutes the Fogo de Chão family.

Giocondo Angeli is a member of this large team of warriors. Currently a director in the United States, he began working at Fogo de Chão in 1987, as a cleaner, and he laughs on recalling the early period in Dallas, when the only road that they knew went from their home to the *churrascaria*: "We were afraid of going out to any different place. We lived close to the restaurant and made our way walking a distance of roughly two miles. To overcome the difficulties and make the business

successful no efforts were spared. We worked 15, 17 hours a day, more than willingly. Communicating in the English language was particularly difficult but to everyone's relief, Selma de Oliveira, a Brazilian native who had already been living in the United States for a long while, joined the team and went on to welcome the customers. The gauchos would serve the food while she dealt with the conversation. At the same time, all of them began to take English lessons and a good number of them, on feeling themselves more confident regarding the language, went on to attend regular schooling. Today, there are no doubts regarding their having decided correctly to face the challenge: the pioneer team saw its efforts succeed and bear fruit. Thanks to this united team, Fogo de Chão became what it is today: a token of efficiency and quality.

[1] The term employed to refer to a boy.

Entering the 21ˢᵗ century on the right foot

Even today, with more than 20 branches spread around Brazil and the United States, Jair and Arri Coser remember the opening dates of each branch. In Brazil, after those of Porto Alegre, Moema and Santo Amaro, they opened the branches on Avenida Bandeirantes, in São Paulo, in October 2003, in Belo Horizonte, in Minas Gerais, in September 2006, then in Brasília, in May 2007, and then in Salvador in 2008.

The branch on Avenida Bandeirantes was born large, the biggest of all of them. Three weeks before its inauguration, the 70 employees hired already rehearsed the "Fogo de Chão *ballet*" on the site, which featured a line out front already as of the first day, and returned the best result ever obtained by the company. In order to be capable of serving the immense clientele, which practically doubled on Sundays, it became necessary to expand the team that today comprises 110 people.

Belo Horizonte, the capital of Minas Gerais, was an old objective of the partners, accustomed to receiving many Minas natives at their São Paulo branches. In addition, the proximity to the São Paulo capital facilitated logistics and, as of 1994, the partners traveled frequently to Minas Gerais in search of a good opportunity. The years of 1994, 1995 and 1996 went by and everything was so expensive, there was no way they could close a deal. Eventually, the opportunity to operate in Dallas, ended up placing Belo Horizonte on the backburner. Installing a branch in the United States required a lot of concentrated breath and energy and meant an immense step in the journey of Fogo de Chão. A step that deserves a special chapter in this history.

In 2006, Fogo de Chão opened in Belo Horizonte, the capital of the State of Minas Gerais

The branches of Santo Amaro, Bandeirantes and Moema in São Paulo, and the ones in Salvador and Brasília, together with the Belo Horizonte branch comprise the Fogo de Chão chain in Brazil

The opening of each new Fogo de Chão branch requires the work of engineers, architects and a large construction team. Below, photos of the building of the Belo Horizonte and Brasília branches

Only in 2006 the branch in Belo Horizonte was inaugurated, in the Savassi suburb. The old desire was revived by Alexandre Fialho who at that time lived in the city. On a trip to Mendoza, in Argentina, Arri became acquainted with the professor of business strategy who was already a customer of Fogo de Chão in São Paulo and advised him to go ahead with the business deal, introducing people to him and advising the gaucho businessmen whenever necessary. At his time the company already had a well-structured human resources division, with an efficient program for the qualification and updating of its employees. With a lot of experience accumulated from their growth in the United States, Belo Horizonte was yet another sto-

ry of success for the partners that would be repeated in Brasília the next year.

Fogo de Chão already attracted customers in Washington, the center of political power in the United States, which then sparked their interest in the capital of Brazil. The branch's opening was a memorable event to its employees owing to the efforts required by them in order to make everything come out as planned. The team of more than 100 people had undergone training over four months and, on arriving in Brasília, found the branch in the finishing-touches. The inauguration date had been set, but there was still work left for another 15 days. The gaucho fighting spirit reared up and on being convoked by the company's director of operations, Jandir Dalberto, the waiters, *maîtres d'*, cleaners, kitchen assistants, gaucho barbecue chefs, managers, and the boss, all rolled up their shirtsleeves and began working hands-on. Literally. Those who were conversant with carpentry were designated to deal with the windows, those who had gardening experience were designated to deal with greenery and thus it went with painting, cleaning and whatever else there was to be dealt with. In four days, the branch was ready, everything spick-and-span. The architect and builder were left speechless. The priest came to say the inauguration mass and asked the Fogo de Chão team to sing, and the gauchos didn't hesitate to sing the Rio Grande do Sul anthem with pride.

And who would ever have thought that the company with roots in the Serra Gaúcha would arrive in Bahia, in Brazil's northeast? The characteristic daring of Fogo de Chão would be a mark of this venture too, and the wager made on a coastal city, with a strong tourist potential, the entry gate to flights arriving from France, Portugal and the United States, proved right. Today, Fogo de Chão is considered a gastronomic reference in the city, together with restaurants offering the regional cuisine, and the *churrasco* coexists in perfect harmony with the Bahian dish, *vatapá*.

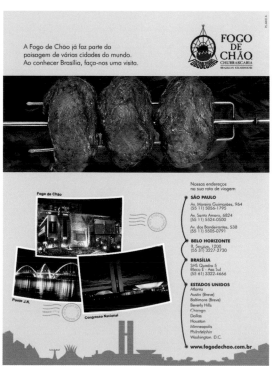

The Fogo de Chão cheese bread: simply delicious!

"But don't you have cheese bread at Fogo de Chão? You've got to have it," said some of the customers. We already offered it at some of the other branches, so we had to have it here as well. But to serve the customers those hard and mealy rolls which took away from the customers stomach the valuable space for yet another succulent piece of meat, only because the market demanded it? No way. Especially because one of the features of Fogo de Chão is its exclusiveness and if it were necessary to add a new product it had to be truly new and with the same quality as the other products served to the customers.

The recipe of the famous cheese bread served at Fogo de Chão, soft, light, unique, did actually emerge from the restaurant's kitchen and, says the legend, because it was so well-liked it has already caused a polemic among natives of the State of Minas Gerais, the origin of cheese bread. Some criticize Fogo de Chão's cheese bread, defending the "legitimate Minas cheese bread." But numerous other fans issue lavish praise, and guarantee that they have never in their homeland been offered a cheese bread as good as that of Fogo de Chão. To check this

out you will have to either visit one of the chain's restaurants or make the cheese bread yourself. Here's the recipe, for roughly 60 units.

Ingredients:
• 12 eggs;
• 1 liter of cooking oil;
• 2 spoons of salt;
• 1 1/2 kg of sweet manioc flour;
• 250 g of sour manioc flour;
• 350 g of grated cheese;
• 1 liter of milk.

Preparation:
• Mix all the ingredients and lastly add the milk.
• Blend in the blender until you obtain a well-homogenized consistency.
• Place the dough in a bread pan and heat in a preheated oven for about 10 minutes at a temperature of 220° and then let it bake for another 20 to 25 minutes.

Chapter 3

Say: shur-ras-kay-ros, a-rose car-ray-tay-ro, pi-can-ya, cos-tell-a. These instructions on how to pronounce the terms *churrasqueiros* (gaucho-style barbecue chefs), *arroz carreteiro* (rice with jerked beef), *picanha* (prime cut of top sirloin), *costela* (beef ribs), written thus in Portuguese, were some of the many hints provided by the restaurant critic of the "The Dallas Morning News," Doty Grifith, under the enthusiastic headline "Brazilian steakhouse is a 'meat-eaters' mecca."

Fogo de Chão
conquers America

Hints designed to enable the customer to appreciate and understand what would be a pleasant contact with the Brazilian gaucho culture by means of a surprising gastronomic experience.

Façade of the Dallas branch in the United States

Washington**Weekend**

Dining Out

Corinna Lothar

Fogo de Chao fans the flame for carnivores

Brazilian fare the gaucho way

The gauchos in their light blue shirts, wide black leather belts and red scarves glide gracefully as a cowboy roping a heifer, moving though the dining room with skewers of meat: beef, pork, lamb, chicken and sausage. Fogo de Chao, the new southern Brazilian churrascaria, serves grilled meat the gaucho way.

The formula is simple, identical at lunch and dinner: guests serve themselves at the salad bar while a waiter brings a basket of warm, divine little cheese rolls to the table (they're addictive). Then, on clean plates, diners are served by the gauchos who come by frequently with 15 different cuts of meat.

Diners control the service with small round paper discs — the green side up means bring on more meat; red means stop for now. You can turn the disc over as often as you like.

Waiters are not assigned to specific tables; if diners want something, they can hail any waiter, who will promptly deal with the request. While this is a good idea for a restaurant of this kind, the number of gauchos and waiters constantly moving about the restaurant promotes a certain quality of restlessness.

Traditionally, Brazilian gau- ... or cowboys, grilled their ... slowly over ...

The new Washington restaurant, on the ground floor of the old Evening Star building on Pennsylvania Avenue at 11th Street Northwest, has been designed by Adamstein & Demetriou. It seats about 350 people, but the large space is cleverly divided by walls of wine bottles and nicely spaced tables. Even when the restaurant is full, it is not overly noisy and it's possible to have ... versation.

In Brazil, we ... is never served ... green. Hence, th ... ditionally Brazil ... Chao, the salad b ... ous. Everything i ... and each bowl is ... whenever it begin ... empty. Beautiful f ... spikes of heart of p ... choke hearts, succu ... dried tomatoes, a cr ... salad similar to tabb ... sciutto, mozzarella b ... salami, smoked salm ... refreshing apple sala ... raisins, crisp greens, ... yellow peppers and an ... mous wheel of Parmes ... cheese are some of the ... ings.

Slices of fresh tomato ... little flavor at this time o ... year, and the potato salad ... bland, but almost everyth ... else is fresh and good. Ev ... thing is pretty and appetiz ... There's no prepared vinaigrette, although olive oil an ... available, and ...

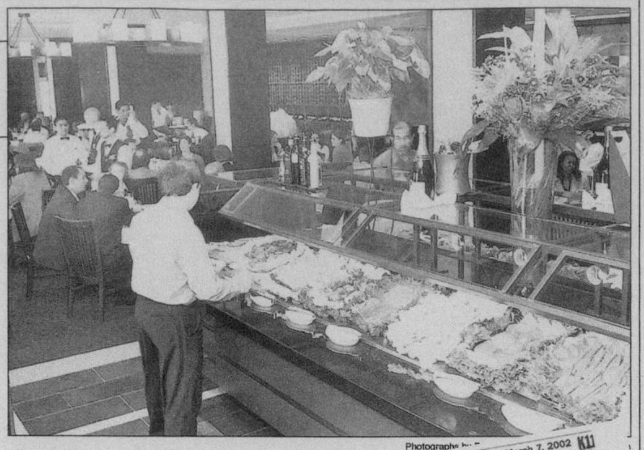

Photograph b...

The meat at Fogo de Chao is not served with anything green, but customers can help themselves to the salads and ... vegetables at the sumptuous buffet ... the rotisserie grill. Th... regul...

The Atlanta Journal-Constitution / Thursday, March 7, 2002 K11

FROM THE MENU OF . . . / FOGO DE CHÃO, 3101 Piedmont Road, Atlanta, 404-266-9988

A Brazilian twist on beans and rice

Q: Fogo de Chão is worth the money and the trip, especially the black beans and rice. I sometimes find myself dreaming about the dish. It's the best I've ever had. Any chance you might be able to get the recipe?

— **Linda Courts,** Smyrna

A: Fogo de Chão, Atlanta's first Brazilian churrascaria, was happy to share this recipe. The rice is made with charque, jerked Brazilian meat also known as carne seca. Charque can be found in Brazilian markets. Bruce Schonholz of Best of Brazil in Marietta and Expedition International Travel in Sandy Springs tells us there is a shortage of this import, but more is expected shortly. Even without it, this dish is loaded with flavorful meats, taking it from side dish to main course.

— **Jeanne Besser,** for the Journal-Constitution

MAIN DISH

Black Beans

Makes 4 servings — Preparation time: 20 minutes, plus overnight soaking — Cooking time: 1 hour

...pound black beans
...spoons vegetable oil
2 pork sausages, sliced
8 ounces pork loin, cut into small cubes
Tabasco, to taste
Salt to taste

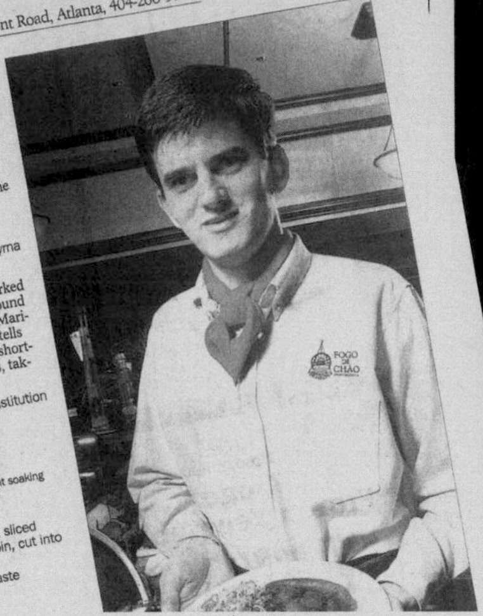

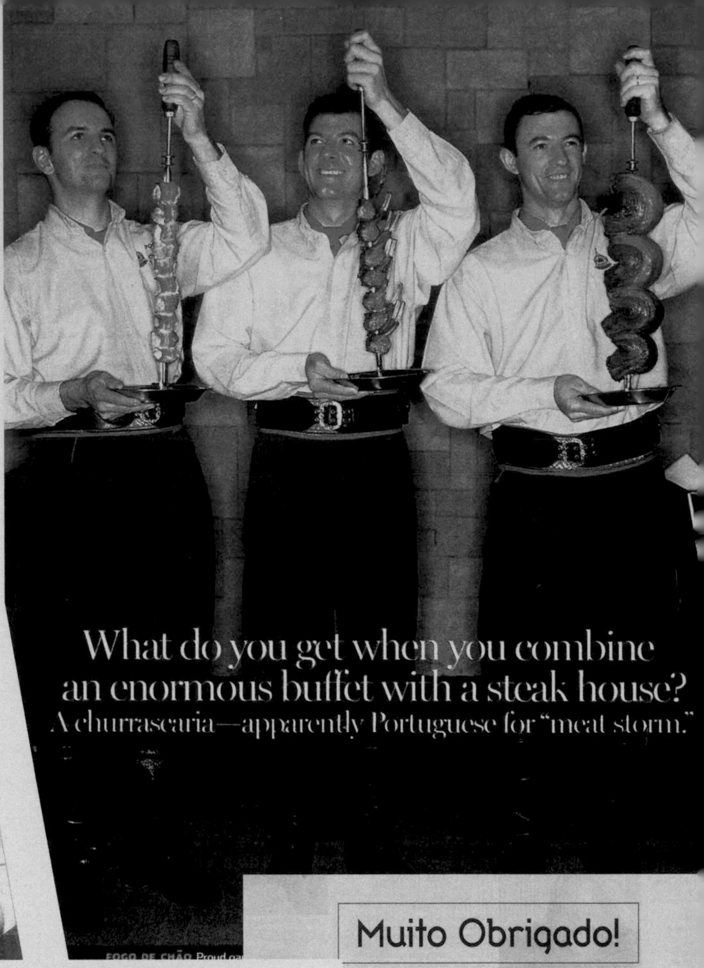
What do you get when you combine
an enormous buffet with a steak house?
A churrascaria—apparently Portuguese for "meat storm."
FOGO DE CHÃO Proud ga...

BRASILEIROS NO EXTERIOR

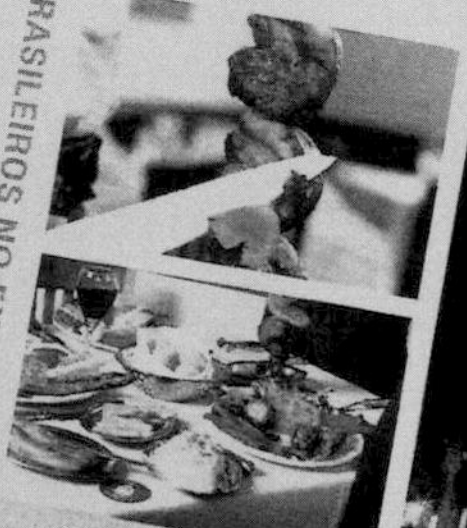

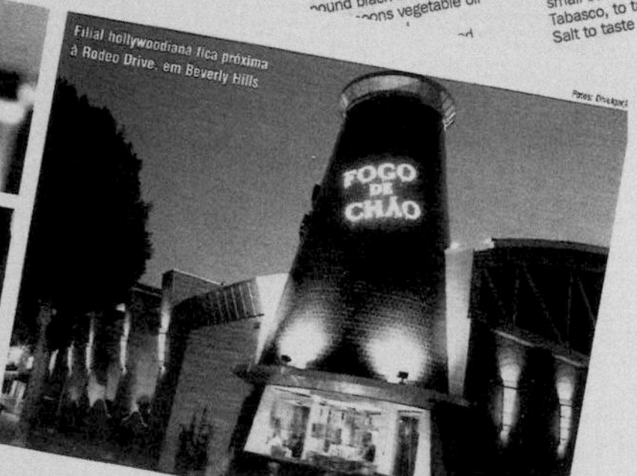
FOGO DE CHÃO

Filial hollywoodiana fica próxima à Rodeo Drive, em Beverly Hills

De Porto Alegre para Beverly Hills

Empresário revela a fórmula do sucesso da churrascaria brasileira que recebe um milhão de americanos por ano

POR LUCIANA TUZINO, DE TORONTO

Em 25 anos, os fundadores da rede de churrascarias Fogo de Chão traçaram uma trajetória de acertos que serve de ...ção para quem sonha em vencer ...gócios.

...mãos Jair e Arri Coser e Aleixo Ongaratto deixaram a Serra em 1976 com o objetivo ...

...certo. Depois de inaugurar sua primeira casa em 1979, um chalé com telhado de palha em Porto Alegre, o quarteto não parou de crescer, abrindo filiais em São Paulo e nos Estados Unidos. Hoje, os irmãos gaúchos comandam nove casas, quatro no Brasil e cinco nos EUA. E não pretendem parar por aqui. O projeto ...

Um dos grandes diferenciais da Fogo de Chão é que lá o churrasco continua sendo a grande estrela, o que significa que o bufê não compete com o rodízio. O ambiente sofisticado é outra marca da rede, que tem uma adega premiadíssi...

FRIDAY DINING

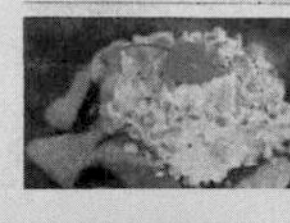

★★★★ OUTSTANDING ★★★ EXCELLENT ★★ VERY GOOD ★ GOOD

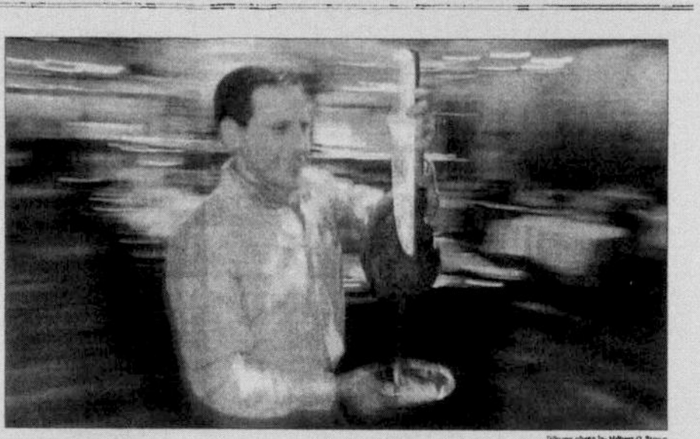

Gaucho servers are fast and efficient with the meats at churrascaria Fogo de Chao

Tribune photo by Milbert O. Brown

REVIEW

Boys from Brazil arrive

Churrascaria-style dining makes debut in Chicago, Schaumburg

By Phil Vettel
Tribune Restaurant Critic

For meat lovers, the concept behind Brazilian *churrascarias* Fogo de Chao and Sal & Carvao — continuous, tableside service of grilled and roasted beef, lamb, pork and chicken for a single, set price — is virtually irresistible.

All-you-can-eat for under $40? Including more than a dozen cuts of meat, presented in a format that requires no consumer decision-making beyond "yes, please" and "no, thank you"?

The question is not "will this concept fly here?" but "what took you so long to get here?"

Fogo de Chao opened a month ago in River North; Sal & Carvao opened in Schaumburg three weeks earlier. That seems to be the principal difference between the two restaurants, which are nearly identical in layout, price and format, right down to the color brochures that help you track what you have and haven't sampled.

Those brochures come in handy, because neither restaurant has a menu. Instead there is *espeto corrido*, or continuous service, of food. Costumed gauchos bearing skewers of meat roam the dining room as their ancestors once roamed the Southern Pampas, eager to slice and serve to whomever requests it.

To summon a gaucho, you need do little more than lift a finger — just enough to flip your laminated-cardboard disk (supplied to each diner, not just to each table) to the green-side-up position. Showing green to a gaucho is rather like showing red to a bull; the gauchos charge over in a flash (more delicately than would a bull, to be honest), offering whatever meat they happen to be carrying. You can even specify the doneness level, though temperature control doesn't approach the precision of a good steakhouse.

When one gaucho leaves, another stops by, and another, and so on until you flip the disk back to red, at which point they leave you alone. When you're ready, flip the disk again and service resumes. Don't be shy about seconds or thirds; Lord knows the gauchos aren't.

Both restaurants offer as many as 15 cuts of meat, about a dozen of which are being paraded around at any given time. Beef dominates the selection; there's flavorful top sirloin, somewhat leaner bottom sirloin, filet mignon (long slices or individual, bacon-wrapped medallions), beef ribs (generally quite fatty) and *picanha*, or rump steak. The *picanha* is as close to a signature cut as you'll find at either restaurant, and it's a terrific piece of meat — juicy and packed with flavor.

Lamb arrives as a whole leg or individual chops. There's whole pork loin, pork loin medallions dusted with parmesan cheese, along with ribs and well-seasoned pork sausage. There are also chicken drumsticks and bacon-wrapped chicken breasts. Conspicuously absent on the menu are the Fred Flintstone brontosaurus ribs, the only cut of meat I believe they overlooked.

Churrasco-style cooking originated with the plains-riding gauchos (cowboys) of Brazil; meats were cooked over open fire pits, and access to spices was somewhat limited. Accordingly, meats at Fogo de Chao and Sal & Carvao are sparingly seasoned. Beef gets a generous sprinkling of rock salt (more generously so at Sal & Carvao) and nothing more, except for perhaps a hint of garlic in the *picanha*. Chicken and pork are marinated; ribs get a minimal dry rub of seasonings.

Fogo de Chao, which has been in the United States for five years (opening first in Dallas before adding Houston and Atlanta locations), has already learned to adapt its cooking to North American tastes; the meats here are not as heavily salted as they would be in Sao Paulo. This is a lesson the Sal & Carvao people should learn; on one of my Schaumburg visits the meats were so heavily salted the differences between the various cuts became merely a matter of texture.

But one does not live by meat alone (although here one certainly could; I think I left one restaurant with a day's worth of protein stuck between my teeth), and so meals include unlimited trips to the salad bar. Both restaurants put out big buffets, loaded with beautifully presented greens, bell peppers, hearts of palm, artichoke bottoms, cheeses, breads and more.

And there are complimentary side dishes as well. First to the table is a plate of *pao de queijo*, addictive little cheese puffs, followed by good mashed potatoes and fried bananas. Beware of these gastric space invaders, for they take up room better saved for the good stuff.

You will not be surprised, at this point, to learn that both restaurants offer the same signature dessert, namely *creme de papaya*, a rich pudding of papaya and ice cream drizzled with some creme de cassis. It's hard to imagine many customers having room for dessert, but if you do, the creme de papaya is a pleasant enough, easily shared sweet.

Both restaurants offer substantial wine lists, heavily weighted toward full-bodied reds and divided among American, South American, European and Australian products. If you've never tasted wines produced in Chile and Argentina, here's an opportunity to do so without breaking anyone's budget.

Service is amazingly efficient; I defy anyone with a green-side-up disk to count to 50 before a gaucho arrives. But beyond the haunch-hacking gauchos, there also are other staffers on the prowl for glasses to refill, side-dish plates to be replenished and so forth. Both do well in this regard, but Fogo de Chao runs a more polished front room by a comfortable margin. The gauchos are nattier-looking and a bit quicker on the draw; servers are lightning-fast with drink refills, quicker to replace used plates with clean ones and more personable overall.

Both dining rooms are warm and inviting. Tables are topped with white linen; dining areas are carpeted. The restaurants attract large parties, but the noise level remains tolerable.

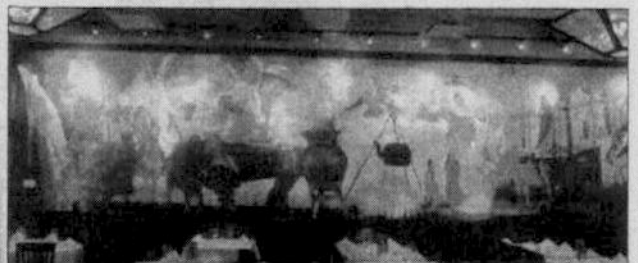

Tribune photo by Milbert O. Brown

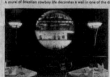

A mural of Brazilian cowboy life decorates a wall in one of the dining rooms at Fogo de Chao.

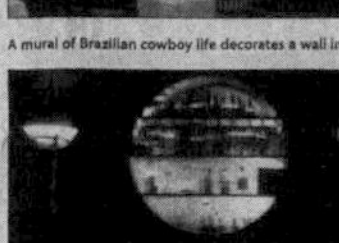

Photo for the Tribune by Peter Thompson

Spacious Sal & Carvao is one of two large churrascarias that have opened in the Chicago area this season.

Fogo de Chao ★ ★
661 N. LaSalle St.
312-932-9330
Open: Dinner Mon.-Sun., lunch Mon.-Fri.
Prices: $38.50 dinner, $24.50 lunch
Credit cards: A, DC, DS, M, V
Reservations: Recommended
Noise: Conversation-friendly
Other: Valet parking
Smoking in bar only

Sal & Carvao ★
801 E. Algonquin Rd., Schaumburg
847-925-0061
Open: Dinner Mon.-Sun., lunch Mon.-Fri.
Prices: $38.50 dinner, $22.50 lunch
Credit cards: A, DC, DS, M, V
Reservations: Recommended
Noise: Conversation-friendly
Other: Complimentary valet parking
Smoking in bar only

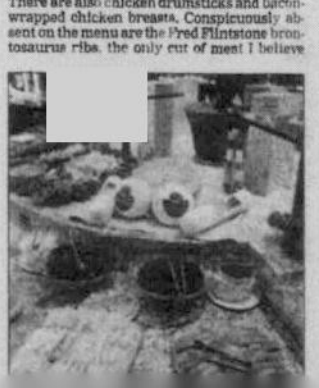

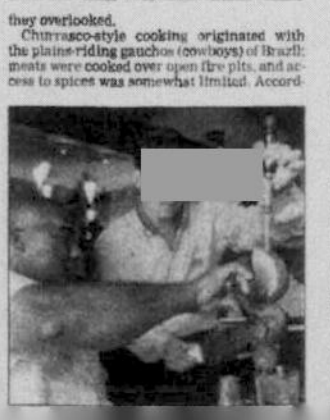

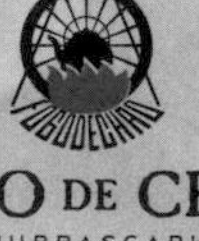

Muito Obrigado!

That's our way of saying "thank you very much". You've help make our first year in the United States a huge success. And coming back to see us, would be your way of saying "de nada".

For reservations call 972-503-7300.
Complimentary valet parking available.

Open for Lunch Mon-Fri 11-2

Dinner Sun-Thurs 5-10
Fri and Sat 5-10:30

FOGO DE CHÃO
CHURRASCARIA

4300 Beltline Road Addison, TX 75244

Santo Amaro, São Paulo — Indianópolis, São Paulo — Porto Alegre

Brazil!

Cultural tapestry celebrated at Houston festival

By DAI HUYNH
Houston Chronicle

Brazil is a land of contrasts.

Tropical rain forests and steamy jungles dominate the north; fertile farmlands and lush grazing areas sprawl across much of the south; and white beaches line the country's long Atlantic coast.

Like the land, Brazil is a vibrant patchwork made up of more than 30 different nationalities, including Europeans, Asians and Africans. This colorful tapestry has given birth to a culinary heritage that's slowly being discovered by diners in the United States.

This is largely due to the Brazilian-style *churrascarias* or steakhouses that have opened around the country in the last couple of years, said Brazilian Ivan Utretra, founder and president of Rodizio Grill.

Houston now has two Brazilian steakhouses, Rodizio Grill and Fogo de Chao, located a few blocks from each other on Westheimer.

And this weekend, Houstonians can learn more about Brazilian food and culture at the 2000 Houston International Festival downtown. The salute to the largest country in South America will showcase traditional Brazilian fare from Clive's downtown and Rodizio Grill. This is in addition to booths spotlighting foods from the Caribbean, China, Africa, Mexico and Italy.

While Rodizio Grill serves skewered meats and Brazilian fruit drinks, Clive's Brazilian Hut will feature such traditional dishes as acaraje com camarao (shrimp and bean fritters with malagueta pepper sauce), xinxim (shrimp and chicken stew with coconut and rice), and fried plantains with cilantro and garlic sauce.

Clive Berkman of Clive's has participated in the Houston International Festival for a decade, offering traditional dishes from the honored country each year.

"We did France, Italy, and last year, South Africa," he said. "Each year, it's like an educational trip. It's fascinating to learn about a country's culture and food. It's like school for me."

But Berkman found himself a little intimidated by Brazil and enlisted the help of consulting chef Hugo Lujamdio, who worked in a Brazilian restaurant.

"This is a first for me (to hire someone to help with the festival)," Berkman said. "But I don't know much about South America, much less Brazil."

Defining Brazilian cooking is difficult.

"There are just so many flavors, so many influences – the Japanese, Greeks, West Africans, Portuguese, Chinese, Lebanese and Germans," Berkman said. "From the standpoint of flavors and ingredients, Brazil has more than any other country, as far as I'm concerned. It's a giant mosaic."

Brazil is slightly smaller than the United States, with about half the population. And like the United States, Brazil's cuisine is the product of both tradition and circumstance. Each region's dishes are rooted in the indigenous culture, which European group colonized the region, proximity to the ocean, annual rainfall and soil conditions.

For example, chilies round out many of the stews and soups in northern Brazil. In contrast, Brazilians in the south rarely use peppers in their cooking. Another major difference: While northern Brazilians prefer to dry their meats in the sun, cowboys or gauchos in the south cook steak on grills like their neighbors in Argentina and Uruguay.

There is a common thread among the regional cuisines, though. Africa gives much of Brazilian cooking its distinguished personality. Nutty palm oil is widely used for frying and in sauces. Coconut is widely used, too, along with both fresh and dried shrimp, yuca, cashews, almonds, bananas and beans.

Brazil is the world's biggest producer and largest consumer of beans. The national dish of Brazil is feijoada à Brasileria, or Brazilian black beans. The dish, available at the Rodizio Grill and the soon-to-reopen Samba Cafe, consists of black beans cooked with dried beef and spareribs. The rich stew is tradi-

See DRAZIL on Page 14G.

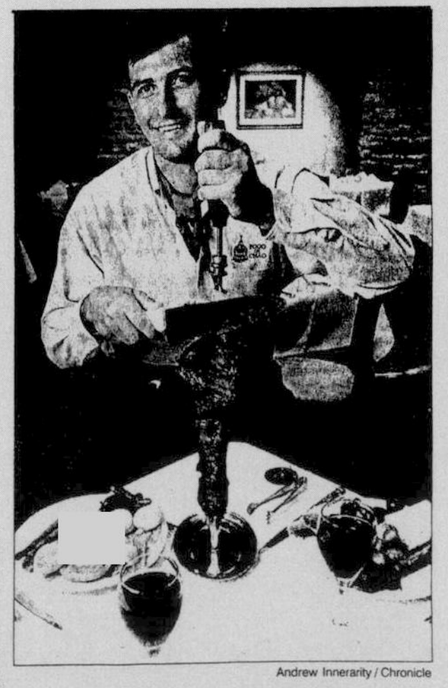

Andrew Innerarity / Chronicle

Lederson Erdma cuts a top sirloin at Fogo de Chao, a Brazilian-style *churrascaria*, or steakhouse

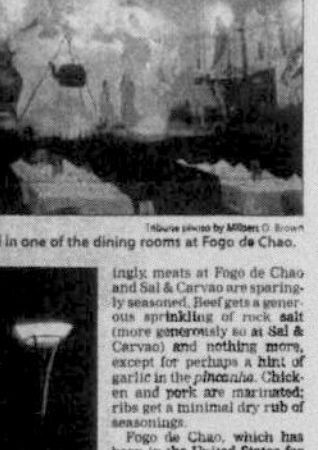

Delight...

South American Steak Houses are ...

by Ann Stone

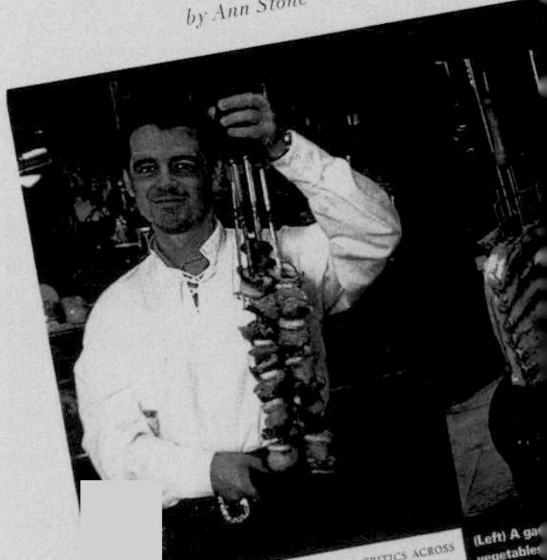

(Left) A ga... vegetable...

Food critics across the nation have long recognized Houston as the restaurant capital of America due to the the abundance of new restaurants opening at warp speed and ... bestowed annually ...

American... Corlu... opened ... walked ... perplex... take H... food...

Fogo de Chão

A FIERY EATING EXPERIENCE

BY NANCY JACQUELINE GARCIA
Photography by Tres Smith

天堂 Fogo de Chão

DE CHÃO
CHURRASCARIA

圖文／維诺

2006年3月4日

Men and meat

Fogo de Chão's herd of beef-toting gauchos brings home the range
By Mark Stuertz

Aside from being situated at opposite ends of the hemisphere, it's hard to imagine what Brazil and Texas have in common. All attempts to uncover harmonious congruence seem to put a gasket-blowing strain on credulity.

Brazil is a geologically integrated nation with a web of rivers and tributaries spread over its irregularly shaped land mass like a mat of thinning hair on a bald spot. Texas is a huge state with a maze of man-made lakes rippling its surface like water-logged nine-iron divots, and borders that look as though they had been drawn by toddlers with Etch-a-Sketches.

Brazil hosted the Earth Summit, where people such as Al Gore and John Denver wallowed in their own green piety and urged everyone to save the world by doing things like: roasting weenies in solar ovens. Texas hosts the Mary Kay convention, where people like Mary Kay urge devotees to get rich and paint their cars Pepto-Bismol pink.

Brazil shares a border with Bolivia, a major producer of illicit narcotics that it ships all over the world. Texas shares a border with Arkansas, a major producer of illicit ethical standards that it ships in bulk to Washington, D.C.

These are just a few of the untidy parallels that can be drawn between these two jurisdictions. Which is why it's interesting that a Brazilian restaurant group decided that Texas—indeed Dallas—was the perfect spot to introduce its specific brand of Brazilian cuisine to Americans. According to Orlando Freissler, general manager of **Fogo de Chão**, a new dining spot on restaurant row in Addison, Texas really does have a lot in common with Brazil, especially with that country's southern region. "There was a reason we came to Dallas," he says. "It's the similarity that Texas has with Southern Brazil. You have the cowboys here, there we have the gauchos. We like meat, just as you people love meat."

Sure, we have cowboys. But ours wear helmets and cleats, use intricate patterns over fat white lines, and lock themselves in motel rooms exploring new ways to develop the market for Bolivian exports. Brazilian cowboys—or gauchos, as they are called—roam the pampas (the vast savanna in southern South America) and herd livestock wearing baggy pantaloons, hand-tooled leather belts and boots, and scarves. These gauchos are the inspiration behind Fogo de Chão.

With two locations in Sao Paulo (the largest city in South America) and one in Porto Alegre, Fogo de Chão is narrowly focused on the churrasco, the gaucho barbecue that incorporates beef, pork, chicken, and lamb. Traditionally, the churrasco begins when an animal is slaughtered on the pampas and pieces of meat are cut and impaled on a metal spit. The spit is then forced into the ground next to a fire at such an angle that the meat hangs over the coals—it's positioned so that it doesn't burn, but roasts slowly. As it cooks, it's basted with a mixture of salt and water.

This traditional gaucho mythology, which calls for the consumption of vast quantities of barbecued meat, is memorialized in the elaborate barbecue silo built into the front of Fogo de Chão (which means "fire of the ground," or campfire, in Portuguese). Encased in thick glass that makes a transition to blue and orange tiles as it rises above the roof line, the cylindrical room holds beef ribs or other cuts of meat that are impaled on long skewers, then arranged in a spiky circle around a small pile of smoldering embers. Several beef above the first and meat is a polished copper hood, which carries the heat and smoke out through the top of the silo.

The dining room tempers this unusual barbecuing structure with contemporary ranch-style touches, including a low wooden lattice ceiling held up by thick, angular wooden pillars. Near the front of the restaurant, the ceiling is vaulted with thick wood beams and planks. The tables are set with heavy Brazilian flatware that has an elaborate gauchos-on-the-pampas scene embedded into thick handles. These settings also include a small pile of tongs.

"We started working as busboys and cleaning floors," explains Jorge Ongaratto. "And we started dreaming about opening our own restaurant."

> It's hard to get away from the fact that everything seems in service to this gaucho gimmick.

gauchos wander around the restaurant with long skewers of chicken, beef, pork, or lamb, looking for places to unload it.

You signal your carnivorous desires with a two-sided disk next to your setting: red for sim não obrigado or no thank you, and green for sim por favor, or yes, please. The gaucho traffic control, however, often isn't smooth. On a number of occasions, our table was approached by skewer-wielding gauchos when there was no green disk in sight. And watch out when you flip it to green, because the skewer traffic at your table will gridlock your appetite. In one instance, a tall blond gaucho (surprisingly, the folks in Southern Brazil have more of a Germanic look than those in the north because of variations in European immigration patterns) sliced us pieces of picanha, a Brazilian cut of beef near the rump. He returned two more times within just a few minutes, not seeming to notice the heap of sliced meat on our plates.

As the gauchos approach a table, they ask if you would like a bit of whatever it is they have on their skewer, which they carry with two hands: one holding the top, the other pressing a small metal drip cup against the tip. They set this cup on the table, and slice off a bit of meat, urging you to clutch the flapping flesh with your tongs as it's cut away from the skewer. The really amazing thing is that on some cuts, the gauchos will ask how you like your meat (rare, medium, or well) and will twirl the skewer to the appropriate spot and cut off a bit of meat with the appropriate hue.

The gauchos control every aspect of the meat's preparation—from its seasoning, to its placement on a special Brazilian grill designed to hold the skewers, to its removal and service. And how is the food overall? On one level, it's hard to get away from the fact that everything seems in service to this gaucho gimmick. A few cuts of meat were fairly good. The bottom sirloin was rich, juicy, and tender—if slightly chewy—with lots of hearty fla-

Continued on page 61

▲ Pantaloon-clad waiters serve meat hot off the spit at Fogo de Chão.

Fogo de Chão:
Dinner $25.50
Lunch $19.50
Salad bar only $15.50

SPECIAL REPORT · HOT CONCEPTS

38 • May 12, 2003

Fogo de Chão

Brazilian churrascaria records beefy sales with style, consistency and service

By Bret Thorn

When most Americans go out to eat, they usually don't say, "Hey, let's go out for some southern Brazilian food," until they've been to Fogo de Chão.

Last year the all-you-can-eat house of meat posted sales of about $48 million as it wowed customers with its style, consistency and great service at four U.S. locations, in Dallas, Houston, Atlanta and Chicago. And by the end of 2003, Californians will join the initiated when a fifth Fogo de Chão opens in Beverly Hills.

The premise is simple. Guests pay a flat rate — from $39.90 in the Texas locations to $43.50 in Chicago at dinner, and around $25 at lunch — and help themselves to the 30-plus-item salad buffet. Then they sit and enjoy the "espeto corrido," or continuous service, of a traditional churrascaria.

Guests use a disk with a green side and a red side at their table to indicate when they are ready to eat. When the green side of the disk is up, servers dressed as gauchos, the South American version of cowboys, surround the table with spits of meat to be carved tableside. The 15 meats range from beef seasoned with sea salt to marinated pork to leg of lamb. Buffet items include fresh mozzarella, hearts of palm, pickles, cold cuts and more.

"It's great," says John Kessler, food critic for The Atlanta Journal-Constitution. "I've been to other churrascarias in other cities and in South America, and [Fogo de Chão] just has great quality control. They've inspired a lot of imitators here. But I don't think any of them have come up as good or as consistent."

Even during the later end of lunch service, Kessler says, the meat is cooked to the temperature you want it. "I've eaten there with very finicky Brazilians, and they've passed the test," Kessler says.

Specialty drinks, including a soft drink called Guaraná and a classic Brazilian cocktail, the Caipirinha, and a full bar are available.

Alcohol accounts for about 20 percent of sales, almost all of it wine, mostly from the United States and Chile. Caipirinhas also are popular at the beginning of meals. Port, officials say.

Children 5 years old and younger eat for free.

The owners and founders of Fogo de Chão are Jair and Arri Coser and Jorge and Alexio Ongaratto, two pairs of brothers from the same farm town in the southern Brazilian state of Rio Grande do Sul. They left home as teenagers to help their fathers, both farmers, pay off bank loans. They got jobs in restaurants.

A few years later in 1979, at the average age of 20, they pooled the money they had saved from tips and opened their first Fogo de Chão in Rio Grande do Sul's capital, Porto Alegre.

That was followed by the opening of two more units in the massive Brazilian city of São Paulo.

"In São Paulo, we have a lot of American business people who travel there," Jorge Ongaratto explains. "And they always say, 'You never thought to go to the U.S.A. with this concept?'"

Eventually they did just that. Since none of the brothers spoke English, they first found a lawyer who spoke Portuguese. He lived in Dallas, so they moved there in 1996.

"Texas was similar to our state, Rio Grande do Sul," Jorge Ongaratto says. "Between the cowboys and the gauchos, there are a lot of similarities. We felt at home."

The brothers say their timing was good. The Brazilian economy was doing well that year and Brazil's currency, the real, was enjoying an unusual period of stability. Thus, they could manage the $3 million needed to buy the land and design and build their restaurant in the Dallas suburb of Addison. Ongaratto puts design and construction costs at around $900,000.

The first U.S. Fogo de Chão opened its doors in August 1997.

"It took the city by storm," says Dotty Griffith, dining editor and restaurant critic of The Dallas Morning News. She cites two reasons for its success. First, "It's very good," she says. Second, it's unusual enough to get people's attention.

"The salad bar is really extraordinary," she adds. "It's very South American-European in the sense that it has all kinds of different olives and pickles and a lot of things you don't see on a traditional American salad bar."

(Continued on page 40)

Meat is Fogo de Chão's main draw. Shown above is the Picanha, sirloin seasoned with sea salt and garlic. Shown at left is the chain's newest unit, which is located in Chicago.

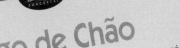

Beef Goes On

t never stops coming at this Brazilian steakhouse chain.

... now the deal with Bra- ... outh American men in ... ndless, phantasmago- ... our table until you cry ... e flag to get them to ... latest upscale steak- ... Harbor, takes that ... e better than your ... out every detail.

... mericas,

... than 30 years, first in Brazil, ... ica. It's

TYLE: Big, bold, upscale chain in the Inner Harbor. **CUISINE:** Brazilian ...tion: meat, meat, and more meat. **YOU'LL FIND:** A wonderland of grilled ...stop to your table by obliging and authentic Brazilian gauchos.

keepers of the flame (literally—Fogo de Chão roughly translates as "campfire"); they're grillmasters who learn the art of barbecue before they can walk, and who take this centuries-old tradition very, very seriously.

Judging from the literature, Fogo's owner—former gauchos themselves—likewise seem pretty passionate about their undertaking. To you and me, it's a steakhouse; to them, it's a mission, one they've been pursuing...

have to say, it pretty well succeeds.

You certainly won't see many churrascarias as elegant as this. The huge space has soaring ceilings, lots of mahogany, white tablecloths, walls lined with wine racks, and a glass-enclosed private dining room. A handsome bar area sits to the left of the entrance, nice for nestling with your caipirinha before the hostess seats you. Despite the place's size, you may indeed have to wait a bit. Fogo has been wildly popular around the country and so far, Baltimore is following suit. It's packed on the weeknight Señor M and I arrive with M's Argentine cousin in tow, although we've barely taken a sip of our cocktails before we're...

—bring skewers of grilled meat

Let's Get Bra...tronogu...

Niche in Houston

FOGO DE CHÃO

El auténtico sabor del Sur de Chão

...o Grill presents skewers of their tasty beef and ...asts on an open pit (churrasqueria) at Fogo de Chão.

...rasco surrounded by maduros and top... with scallions and cotija cheese; and I... ta de Churrasco con Salsa de Jerez y S... butter-like beef tenderloin tips baste... Chimichurri, char-grilled and toppe... dry Spanish sherry, button mushr... and cream. (Churrascos, 2055 West... (at Shepherd). [713] 527-8300; 970... heltner (at Gessner). [713] 952-19...

...OTEIN ...OWER

...N BY MERRILL SHINDLER explores a carnivore's paradise ...ROM BRAZIL IN BEVERLY HILLS. PHOTOS BY GINA SABATELLA.

...urrascaria Fogo de Chão is a monument to meat in the ... the beefiest section of Beverly Hills. A few doors north is Morton's of Chicago, where well-heeled diners luxuriate in the joys of prime steak fast-cooked over grills hot enough to smelt iron. Across the street is Lawry's the Prime Rib, where generations of locals have flocked for a family meal of salad flavored with bottled dressing and meat sliced on rolling carts the size of Cadillac Escalades. The Porterhouse Bistro is around the corner. And yet, no one does meat like Fogo de Chão, where an entire kitchen is dedicated to protein, cooked in a fashion that dates back 500 years or more.

The original branches of Fogo de Chão are in Brazil— three in São Paulo, one in Porto Alegre. In 1997 the first North American Fogo opened in Dallas, followed by outposts in Houston, Atlanta, Chicago, and now Beverly Hills. And though all the Fogos are dramatic structures, the chain opted to throw everything they had at their first effort in Beverly Hills. It's become an instant landmark...

In the preceding pages, the American press praises the resounding success of Fogo de Chão in the United States. Above, the home of the first American Fogo de Chão branch, in Dallas

The year was 1997 and Fogo de Chão—say "fogo-dée-shown," meaning fire on the ground—recently installed in Dallas, was the first branch of a chain of the brand's restaurants in the United States. Now, how did the *churrascaria*, a Brazilian gaucho-style steakhouse, founded by gauchos in the interior of the State of Rio Grande do Sul end up in Texas? Early in the decade of the 1990s, the partners bet on the growth of their business in Belo Horizonte, the capital of the State of Minas Gerais. However, although they traveled a lot to this city in search of a good business deal, they were unable to find a spot that would satisfy their expectations. At the same time, a new economic plan launched by the government, the Real Plan, placed the Brazilian currency on a level quite close to that of the dollar, and real-estate properties in São Paulo were being sold at prices similar to those in the United States. This was sufficient reason to turn the partners' attention to doing business abroad, thinking of the next step to be taken.

Customers and friends always discussed with the owners of Fogo de Chão the possibility of seeking business beyond Brazil's frontiers: France, Italy, Portugal... Several exploratory trips were made to Chile and Argentina, but in 1990, when a friend invited Arri Coser to ski in the United States, all doubts concerning the right destination for the Fogo de Chão investments ceased. "I was taken with the country, by the way things worked, by the economy..." recalls Arri.

To begin with, the idea was to do business in New York, because at the time New York was the place everybody spoke about, but in their search for meat producers the businessmen ended up arriving in Texas. Traveling around the state by car, in the company of Arri, it became Jorge Ongaratto's turn to be enticed by the place. The partner recalls that Jorge was highly impressed by the petroleum pumps seen everywhere, as well as the large number of cattle, so much so that he stated: "Man, this is the Rio Grande do Sul of the Americans. This is where I'm going to settle down." And he did!

Once again, Fogo de Chão found itself at the right place, at the right time. The Brazilian currency's appreciation was extremely favorable to investments outside the country. Another factor that contributed to the venture's success was the personal contact that the partners had established with Eduardo Leite, who represented in Latin America Baker & McKenzie, the

Photo of the historical trip made by Arri Coser and Jorge Ongaratto (above, center) to Dallas, when they found the perfect spot to open their restaurant

At the top, entirely transformed, the site occupied earlier by a Chinese restaurant now housed Fogo de Chão, a novelty that came from afar. And had come to stay. Above, in the restaurant's kitchen, Jair and Larry Johnson, a professional and essential partner in the success of Fogo de Chão in the United States

world's largest law firm. Under Eduardo's guidance, the gauchos came into contact with attorney Larry Johnson—at the time the partner of Baker & McKenzie—who had lived for two years in Brazil and therefore spoke Portuguese and was conversant with the Brazilian culture. The contact was made in 1996, when the gauchos arrived with an advertising portfolio of their company, saying: "This is Fogo de Chão, this is what we know how to do. The rest is up to you!"

Larry Johnson's experience proved very important throughout the entire process of installing the restaurant. He oriented the Brazilian businessmen in the mapping of their market, the hiring of a public relations firm, an architect, a real-estate agent, the search for a site, the preparation of the company contract, the transfer of professionals, in short, everything. After all, from the language to the customs, to the

Jair Coser, who in 1997 headed for the United States, fulfilling his successful goal of opening new avenues for the business

laws, everything in all stages of the operation was foreign to them.

Working with a company of Fogo de Chão's size at the time was an exception to Baker & McKenzie, which was accustomed to providing legal services for large corporations only. But Larry was very happy about his acquaintance with these entrepreneurs who had come from Brazil and who, contrary to the opinion of those who thought their venture wouldn't be successful, went ahead with the business. Larry foresaw a promising future for the gauchos' undertaking.

They had already experienced the bold step of implementing the company's branches in distant and unknown locations. Such as in Porto Alegre and São Paulo which were highly successful investments although there was still the possibility of an unfavorable outcome.

Jair Coser left for Dallas in 1997, investing in the goal to thrive in that bountiful country, with large and diversified markets. Without speaking the language, far away from his roots, he faced the challenge of taking up a new homeland. But for a man who while still very young had left the security of the paternal home in the interior of Rio Grande do Sul to set out on his own path, this was merely one more step — although a large one to be sure.

Proudly, Jair Coser remembers that moment which required great courage and determination: "... It only worked out because the people who left had as their purpose: not to return having suffered failure. And they made things happen, contrary to so many others who had also left, but without having defined a purpose, ended up unable to stay." And he makes a point of emphasizing that the differentiating factor in the operation was the team that faced this challenge rather than the favorable economic situation owing to the Brazilian currency's appreciation.

The entrepreneur today laughs on recalling how much the lack of knowledge of the language made the beginnings of the business difficult. Like the other gauchos "exported" to the United States to work to-

Placed at each table in the restaurant, the paper cards signal the waiters whether or not the customer wants to be served. The novelty pleased the American customers

ward the success of Fogo de Chão's new project, Jair didn't speak English. The feeling of confidence of those who had studied a little English in Brazil disappeared in the first contacts with the Americans' fluent speaking of their own language. In addition to understanding only little and hardly managing to communicate, the team of Brazilians also faced the important task of explaining to the new clientele the restaurant concept they were introducing, since there was nothing in the United States that was similar to Fogo de Chão.

DALLAS, TEXAS
Dallas at night during the flood of May 1990.
Photo by Steve Carson

J-130

Eu estou mandando este cartão de natal
Jorque (os fila tá curto) e este é de cortezia.

Jorge P.g. 96.

I Belive, this citty is verry
Good Pleace to Steak house
I'm alome here, But a I'm Happy
Becouse I think We going to have
Verry Verry Much. Sucess. Here
Here

A-W Distributor and Importers, P.O. Box 154123
Irving, Texas 75015-4123

POST CARD

Feliz natal
Jru você pro jain
e familias.
É que nós tenhamos
uma ano de Sucesso
Sucesso

Me manca de Parole Jer descrivere (com poucos) Aqui
quanto yo jenso que tutto va bene sui fracassos.) e Ali

SPACE RESERVED FOR U.S. POSTAL SERVICE

Desculpe mas eu misturo as
Letras Jorque eu estou ficando Troglodita

US TX 845
John Hinde Curteich Inc.
Printed in Ireland

0 90811 12347 0

Postcard sent by Jorge Ongaratto to his family, in which the gaucho native indicated how he was turning into a true polyglot

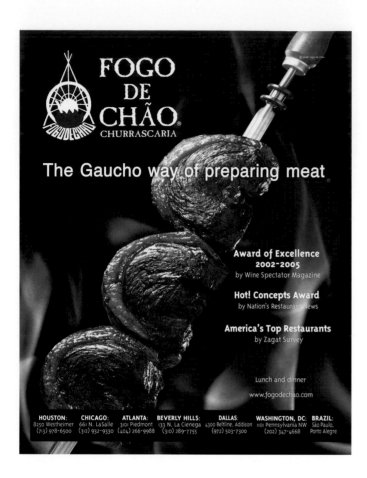

In addition to the authentic gaucho way of preparing the meats, all of the Fogo de Chão restaurants in the United States offer the same cozy ambiance as those in Brazil

But don't you have a menu? How's that possible?

"Imagine a place where on turning over a simple paper card (red on one side and green on the other) you are capable of coordinating a procession of waiters, who carry 15 kinds of different cuts of meat to serve to you on your plate, which will be replenished as many times as you wish... This is the gastronomic orgy dreamed by Henry the VIII come true, yes!?" This short excerpt of an article published in a magazine shows the impact of the novelty that had been installed in a property formerly occupied by a Chinese restaurant, owned by a large grain company in the United States, which had also invested in restaurants.

The location was good and the installations didn't require any hefty investment to transform them into a Fogo de Chão gaucho-style steakhouse. The kitchen was ready, as was the air conditioning and the entire basic structure. All that was lacking was to redo the dining room's decor and, part of the kitchen before opening the doors to the public. The architect responsible for personalizing the new spot traveled to Brazil to become acquainted with the standard of the Fogo de Chão branches and apply to it at the Dallas branch. The challenge was to carry out successfully

an operation that in Brazil had already been mastered by the chain's team of employees in a place where everything was different, from the labor relations to the building material.

Aleixo and Arri remained in Brazil. Jair and Jorge established themselves in Dallas and oversaw the entire preparation process until the branch's opening on August 19, 1997, a day of considerable anxiety. If all beginnings are accompanied by a measure of apprehension, what is one to say of the beginning in which everything was really new, practically a box of surprises?

The first customers entered the restaurant slightly distrustful, they wanted to check out, after all, what this Fogo de Chão was. They usually entered and asked for the menu and received the answer: "Menu? We don't have a menu." It was necessary to explain the system, completely different from what the customer was accustomed to. Giocondo Angeli, today a director of the restaurant chain in the United States, recalls that several times, even after the explanation in "English" given with a measure of difficulty, if the customer stood up to go to the restroom, the waiter kept an anxious eye on him to see whether he didn't actually leave the premises being overwhelmed by so much innovation. Inspired by this day-to-day experience, an explanatory folder was created and is even today placed on each table, explaining the cuts of meat and the service provided.

After four or five months of operation, there was already a line at the entrance to the restaurant, the result of a lot of concerted effort. In addition to the effort invested in the moving and

The core ingredient in the Fogo de Chão recipe for success: the attention paid to the smallest details

Specifications and standards translated into quality

Maximum quality is the guiding motto in all the stages that concern products at Fogo de Chão: ranging from the purchasing of the raw materials to the dish served to the customer. All tested, approved, photographed and systematized so as to conform to the company's specifications at each one of its branches.

The fruits served, for instance, are always of the same kind and are chosen by the buyer observing a predetermined criteria of size, weight and ripeness. Just like the asparagus which is always purchased according to similar specifications. The attention paid to the way the products are grown and stored is a major concern of Fogo de Chão in order to ensure that the foods are put to their best use. Meats, salads and desserts: all of them are subject to a predetermined standard and to quality controls.

In addition to the professional who does the weekly purchasing, the chain's director of operations regularly visits the supply center, being attentive to any innovation in terms of product improvements. By means of fairs oriented toward the segments of supermarkets and restaurants Fogo de Chão keeps up to date and remains in contact with the producers who, fully aware of the customer's great value, may even develop specific products to meet the customer's requirements.

To find the best possible products, company employees travel around the world experiencing everything, seeking excellence and perfection.

The Fogo de Chão branch in Houston

installations, some adaptations were implemented in the course of these months, always seeking to cater to the customer's preference. The cuts of meat, the same as those consumed in Brazil, were approved by the American public, but the quantity of salt was diminished, and the seasoning was given a touch of pepper, entirely in agreement with the Texan taste. And the top sirloin steak was an absolute success right from the start!

Fogo de Chão makes Brazil known across the United States

The operations director of Fogo de Chão in the United States, Selma de Oliveira, had already lived in the country more than ten years when the Brazilian company arrived. Knowledgeable of the market and with the American way of life, she was surprised at the daring of the recently-arrived entrepreneurs and remembers the ease with which Jair Coser affirmed his aggressive expectation, based on expenditure, sales and employee compensation goals. The determination and confidence acquired by means of experience gained in the market would make a reality of this looking toward the future. Jair Coser would bring to the vast American market the keen business vision that had already turned Fogo de Chão into a success in its country of origin.

The Dallas branch was soon doing swimmingly and the partners were already seeking other possible markets in which to implement Fogo de Chão. They opted for Houston, the largest

Carnivore's *Delight*

South American Steak Houses are Carving a Niche in Houston
by Ann Stone

FOOD CRITICS ACROSS the nation have long recognized Houston as the restaurant capital of America due to the the abundance of new restaurants opening at warp speed and the accolades and awards bestowed annually to established institutions.

And, when it comes to innovation, Houston, once again, takes top honors. Although our many existing Texas steakhouses are without peer, we have introduced a new, very specialized version: the South and Central American steakhouse.

CHURRASCOS

MICHAEL CORDUA PIONEERED THE CONCEPT in Houston with the establishment of several immensely successful South

American-style restaurants.

Cordua's first restaurant, Churrascos, opened in 1989. When the first customer walked in and read the menu, he looked perplexed, and walked out. But, it didn't take Houstonians long to discover the great food, served in the warm, comfortable atmosphere of a hacienda. It became so popular, in fact, that another Churrascos opened near downtown in 1990 with the same inviting interior and menu.

Both restaurants offer the same menu, which includes specialties such as Pechuga de Pollo Bahia: grilled breast of chicken with tomatoes, hearts of palm, and cilantro in coconut milk; Gallo Pinto con Carne: black beans and rice stir fried with onions, bell peppers, and shredded Chur-

(Left) A gaucho from Rodizio Grill presents skewers of their tasty beef and vegetables. (Above) Beef roasts on an open pit (churrasquería) at Fogo de Chão.

rasco surrounded by maduros and topped with scallions and cotija cheese; and Puntas de Churrasco con Salsa de Jerez y Setac: butterflied beef tenderloin tips basted with Chimichurri, char-grilled and topped with dry Spanish sherry, button mushrooms, and cream. (Churrascos, 2055 Westheimer (at Shepherd), [713] 527-8300; 9705 Westheimer (at Gessner), [713] 952-1988)

AMERICAS

CORDUA'S SECOND VENTURE, AMERICAS, features gourmet North American, Central American, and South American cuisine. It won *Esquire* magazine's coveted "Best New Restaurant in the United States" award in 1993, the year it opened, and has been collecting awards ever since.

WHERE HOUSTON / JUNE 2000

18

The interior of the Houston branch shows references to the gaucho culture, the foundation of all the work carried out at Fogo de Chão

city in the State of Texas, which hosts a large industrial center in addition to one of the country's busiest ports. The new branch opened its doors to the public in February 2000 and, with the experience acquired in Dallas, the entire process was considerably quicker.

Basically, the American laws were no longer the great unknown, and the many difficulties that had been faced in Dallas did not hamper the business' implementation in Houston. In the list of restaurants elected by the readers of the Houston Business Journal, in April 2001, Fogo de Chão already appeared as the champion in the "Best New Restaurant" category. And there were many reports highlighting the quality of the products, the excellence of the service and the curious fact that the waiters had traveled more than 5,000 miles in order to help spread the tradition of the *espeto corrido*, translated from the Portuguese as the "continuous service," while dressed in *bombachas*, the baggy gaucho-style pants, boots, a blue shirt and red scarf.

Responsible in the United States for the architectural design and for the building of the branches, Fernando Barreto and Cliff Maillet, with the collaboration of the Brazilian architect José Antônio Henrique, who was responsible for the architectonic pattern of the Brazilian branches, suggested that more typical Brazilian features be introduced to the design

In Brazil, as in the United States, typically dressed gauchos prepare the dining room, the meats, and welcome and serve the customers

of the buildings, while maintaining some characteristics of the local architecture, but including the Brazilian ambiance, particularly of the gaucho universe. A restaurant serving typical food, with customs and traditions rooted in its service and a great pride due to its being above all gaucho and first and foremost Brazilian, had to reflect this personality in its installations, and lastly, should be recognized as a sort of "Brazilian embassy." The proposal was promptly accepted by the partners who had never economized investments in actions that would translate into an improvement of the business' quality and image.

Although being a Brazilian, Barreto did not have sufficient knowledge about the gaucho culture, nor about the branches of the Fogo de Chão, and therefore left on a research trip that began

with a visit to all the chain's branches in São Paulo and extended to Porto Alegre, where he got to know the first branch. On this trip Fernando Barreto gathered images, material employed in the construction, typical architectonic and artistic components, in short, an ample baggage that enabled him to better present the gaucho style to the customers in the United States. The warmer colors and even the floor flagged with Brazilian stones and the granite salad buffet tables also brought over from Brazil, formed an ambiance standard at the American branches, based on this emphasis given to the culture from the south. Murals with images originating in Rio Grande do Sul were exhibited on the walls, offering the customer a sort of journey across this Brazilian state, the cradle of Fogo de Chão.

Perfection is the goal

Moema, Beverly Hills, Chicago, Santo Amaro, Denver, in any Fogo de Chão branch the client is received and served as if he were having a meal at his customary Fogo de Chão, in the branch in which he usually takes his business lunch, eats with his family or celebrates an important occasion. The company's effort to make its customers feel as if they are the "Lord of the Hearth," being in charge of their own service, is reflected in the work done on the standardization of products and services, always keeping

in mind the best quality. Thus, the branch's entire employee team has mastered down to the smallest details what the branch has to offer. The team knows each product served, moves about the restaurant's areas with full self-assurance and is even informed about the preferences of the most frequent customers.

To this end, the qualification of the chain's employees involves a training program that comprises general courses offered to the entire team, specific courses relative to the functions performed, updating activities and internal relations, all of which include various teaching materials such as manuals dealing with procedures, the preparation of dishes, and even body language. Language courses are outsourced, but the entire methodology, as well as the training program, was developed by and is regularly updated at the company itself. All of which goes to shape the veritable "choreography" that can be seen daily at each Fogo de Chão branch, in which harmony and efficiency are fundamental. A display of lightness, in which nothing occurs by happenstance and that is even respectfully called the "Fogo de Chão *ballet*." Everything is thought out, subjected to training and closely followed according to a managerial model.

The psychologist Regina Ramos was a Fogo de Chão customer when she was invited to become a member of the company's employee team, in view of the need to prepare professionals to work in the front team in the United States. To deal with the difficulties found abroad, it was necessary not only to qualify but also to identify among the branch's employees those whose profile was appropriate to the situation: to respond to the challenge of moving from one country to another and of taking part in achieving the aim of building up the Fogo de Chão brand among the American public. Implementing a methodology for the selection and training of professionals with a potential for growth and leadership, which resulted in a process at the time referred to as "Training of Leaders," the psychologist launched the seed of what was to become the qualification methodology for the company's human resources.

By the year 2003, the management had structured the areas of human resources, recruitment and selection, personnel training and development of training material, besides the company's managerial model itself, according to which the branch's manager is the overall leader in every sense, qualified to select and train his team more efficiently. Participation in talks and other activities principally connected with the quality of customer service went on to become a routine of the employees. Specific training relative to products, besides general knowledge of themes such as politics, culture and the economy, are part of this constant employee recycling.

Since the company grew and planned to grow additionally, the management implemented a program for the training of multipliers, who not only conveyed knowledge but also carried out an effective quality control. A number of training and standardization materials were developed of both the raw materials destined to prepare the menu and of the manner of preparation and presentation, all of which illustrated with photographs, up to the stage in which the product is finalized and served. In the course of years of experience, including both mistakes and successes, much had been observed and altered, but the systematization of this knowledge occurred at that moment through the first of what today is a series of manuals.

The preparation process of these manuals included *churrasqueiros*, waiters, in short, all the segments involved in the service provided to the customer, making use of the experience of each one of them, encouraging the team to improve the work and establish greater synergy among the branches.

The "Fogo de Chão *ballet*, for instance, became the same for each one of the branches, surprising the customers even more owing to its efficiency and discretion. Concern for the tone of voice and the moving about in the dining room was systematized in a manual of conduct and signals, enabling the constant communication during the serving of customers, in a manner imperceptible to the customer. That is the reason for the customer's surprise at the speed with which the beef ribs ordered from a waiter close by the customer arrive at the table without the waiter's having to move away from the table. Each object, each product, each occurrence is communicated by miming, in a sort of alphabet of gestures mastered by the entire team.

In the same manner, the management standardized the waiters' ordering of dishes, optimizing the understanding between the waiter and the person in charge of the cash register, avoiding possible mistakes. In any branch of the chain the waiter orders a juice or a dessert in the same manner, according to the same procedure. This systematization enables Fogo de Chão to always offer the customer greater quality at a better cost.

In 2006, based on all of this material, the company prepared the "Knowledge Management" project, which ensures the chain's identity and translates its search for excellence and concern for continued training. As tools of the project the management implemented meetings in which the *maître d'* is the multiplier of knowledge, with talks given by suppliers on their products, with specific courses such as that of English, of wines, and others that address the concern with communication, cultural training, acquisition of general knowledge and personal development.

All the themes connected with the Fogo de Chão universe are, in one way or another, dealt with by the employee team in a standardized manner, ensuring that the information arrives equally understood at all the branches.

Fogo de Chão proves
that it is here to stay

The targeted growth of Fogo de Chão in the American territory was converted into a strategy. A country with so many possibilities compelled the group to engage in a constant traveling about to survey new markets. That was how Fogo de Chão made it to Atlanta, in the State of Georgia, where the doors of yet another branch were opened in 2001.

The Chicago branch was inaugurated in 2002 with immense success. One of the world's largest business centers and also a purchasing hub in the American Midwest, this city in the State of Illinois received the restaurant chain with open arms, with lines forming at the door right from the start. Fogo de Chão turned into an event, which won important space in the press and television media. This novelty that came from so far away surprised the American customers who in turn surprised the branch's employees.

Los Angeles was yet another bold move by the company which headed for the country's West in 2005. Here, the Fogo de Chão brand and the *espeto corrido* system were still unknown. The conquest of the Beverly Hills clientele was a challenge that, once overcome, brought significant results to the company in terms of publicity, particularly owing to the strong Los Angeles-New York integration centered on the entertainment industry: the cinema, theater and show business. The first step

A star among stars and other celebrities, the Beverly Hills Fogo de Chão

To the left, in the Austin branch, the beef ribs are shown roasting in the grilling cabinet installed in the façade, the hallmark of all the Fogo de Chão establishments. Below and on the page at right, a view of the dining room of the Washington, D.C. branch

was to show the universe of customers that the aim of the restaurant chain was to offer quality rather than quantity. Differently from what was the common view of a Brazilian *churrascaria* at the time, Fogo de Chão served healthy and first-rate products and brought to Beverly Hills the most attractive salad buffet of Los Angeles. In less than a year, the restaurant became known as a token of excellence to the artists, movie industry executives, tourists from all over the world and many other interesting people.

Strategically, before the end of 2005, Fogo de Chão installed its branch in Washington D.C., the headquarters of the United States government, and one of the world's most important political centers, gaining even greater visibility and national prominence. The subsequent year, Fogo de Chão arrived in Philadelphia, in the American Atlantic coast and, in 2007, another three branches were opened in Minneapolis, Baltimore and Austin. And the aim is to keep on growing.

On the façades of the American branches, the unmistakable feature of the Fogo de Chão chain. Above, from top to bottom: the Beverly Hills branch, opened in May 2005; Washington, D.C. and Philadelphia, inaugurated in December 2006. To the right, two photos of the Baltimore branch, inaugurated in 2007

Above, Minneapolis, inaugurated in 2008 and, to the right, the entrance to the Austin branch

Fogo de Chão in Indianapolis, inaugurated in may 2008

The Kansas branch inaugurated in
2009, and Austin, in 2007

Time for changes

In the midst of the intense expansion process, the brothers Jorge and Aleixo Ongaratto decided to invest in other ventures, leaving the partnership. In order to evaluate the business with indisputable transparency, they contracted with a bank and, in the end, Jair and Arri Coser decided to purchase the share belonging to their partners.

The banking institution that gave them advice suggested that they survey the market, seeking a new partnership for the expansion process. On the reference of a friend, the GP Group contacted Jair and Arri, who were enthusiastic about the idea to have them as partners. This was the largest investment fund in Latin America and the gaucho entrepreneurs were attracted to their style of doing business. In August 2006, GP acquired part of the company.

In January 2007, at the end of many talks, Larry Johnson, the attorney who advised them during the entire process of the Dallas branch's installation, joined Fogo de Chão as its CEO in the United States, showing full confidence in the company's potential and in the work performed by Jair and his carefully assembled team of coworkers.

Wines are given a place of prominence at Fogo de Chão

Roughly 20 years ago, the customer of Fogo de Chão was offered a modest selection of wines. Highly modest, in fact, without any manner of comparison with today's award-winning wine. At that time, some eight or nine labels were offered, most of which were national brands, and the sale of a slightly more expensive bottle was the reason for celebration. There was no good offer available in the market nor was it the custom in Brazil to drink a good wine with the *churrasco*. But Arri Coser, listening to hints made by his friends, began to put into practice the idea of betting more on wines. And it wasn't his friends alone – the customers too requested the introduction of good labels.

Eventually, the company made contact with an importer and bought a good wine menu. This was the beginning move of what was to become a wine cellar reference standard that would reach beyond Brazil. But this didn't develop overnight, although the management soon perceived that the demand was real and the investment was appropriate. The installation of the first wine cellars was praised. These were mobile cellars that allowed the wine to arrive at the customer's table at the proper temperature. Shortly afterwards, on the advice of a professional connoisseur, the wine list was redone and the management launched a process for the service team's qualification by means of tastings and talks.

The experience in the United States, where the consumption of wine is much larger, made the management additionally improve its wine list and service. Today, at all the branches in Brazil, professionals trained by the Brazilian Association of Sommeliers are part of the service team, and the wine list, which comprises roughly 350 labels, has won awards over consecutive years as one of the world's best by Wine Spectator and other prestigious publications. At each branch there is a climate controlled wine cellar especially designed for the dining room's space and the inclusion of a new label is done subject to strict criteria, not only in the tasting but also in the cost analysis, with the aim of doing good business and offering the customer the best options. Every 30 to 60 days, for instance, Fogo de Chão promotes a selection of wines from different regions and offers them to the customers as the "Wines of the Month," which end up arriving at the table at an affordable price.

Always opening new fronts

From the experience obtained with the installation of successive branch restaurants there results a methodology that applies to the company's different segments, simplifying the complexity of the operations comprised in this process: the finding of a promising market, the hiring and training of the employee team, the building of the installations, contracting of national and local suppliers, preparation of contracts, and advertising the company, among several other stages.

The search for new market niches for a restaurant with the characteristics of Fogo de Chão continues under the responsibility of Jair Coser, as well as the identification of the best location for the branch, taking into account especially the ease of access for those who are on a working trip, taking part in an event or simply on a leisure trip. Once the location has been defined, the operational management dedicates itself to get to know the new market up close, making direct contacts with the sector's professionals, with public relations companies, interviewing the available labor force, preparing a diagnosis in order to understand what the region's customers appreciate and what are their expectations relative to a steakhouse, and the specific characteristics of that market.

At the same time, the building team works on the installations and an operational group travels to the location to give all the support required for its opening and its first month of

Closing with a flourish

Just as happens with the meats, salads, and wines, the desserts have always been good, ever since the beginnings of Fogo de Chão. And, of course, in regard to the desserts as well, Fogo de Chão sought to achieve excellence, seeking inspiration at restaurants from several countries worldwide to create new dishes that would meet the high standards of the branch's menu, hiring a chef especially to develop them and keep his recipes secret for a time long enough that they would be identified as products exclusive to Fogo de Chão. In spite of the success of such desserts as the Papaya Cream served with cassis liqueur, Fogo de Chão continues to surprise its customers with novelties.

And to end the gastronomic experience with a flourish, there is the gourmet coffee prepared by a barista especially trained to maintain the high standard of its flavor — he serves a highly special beverage indeed!

operation. Subsequently, this support continues to be provided by the central office in Dallas, headed by Jair Coser, comprising the central structure of accounting, accounts payable and national contracts, besides advice on local negotiations.

With Fogo de Chão's standardized menu, the management today knows exactly which are the products required, and the vendors of the different regions already seek to get acquainted with the company's specifications in order to be able to supply so attractive a customer. Even the publicity and launching arrangements take advantage of the know-how and of the clientele gained.

In 2008, the chain inaugurated another four branches, in accordance with its aim to break into new markets in the country and installing its operations in cities with differentiated profiles and that were very attractive in terms of consumption potential: Indianapolis, in the State of Indiana—principally famous for its motor-racing circuit—Miami, in Florida—an important tourist center—and Scottsdale, in the State of

Arizona. In the beginning of 2009, Fogo de Chão arrived in Kansas City and, in that same year, inaugurated the branches of Denver and San Antonio. Differently from many other businesses which held back on investments in view of the economic crisis that hit the world and, particularly, the United States, the company has maintained its policy of investing in its growth and strength, believing that with the normalization of consumption it will be well positioned to meet consumer demand throughout the country. Today, Fogo de Chão employs more than 1,300 people in the United States, which means that the company has become large even in terms of American standards.

In the United States, as in Brazil, it is normal for people to feel truly welcome at Fogo de Chão, becoming friends of the house. Friends who are received as such, in both the restaurant of their choice and in any other Fogo de Chão branch worldwide. What's the secret? There is no secret. It's a question of a lot of hard work, a serious approach to the business and, above all, quality.

Dados Internacionais de Catalogação na Publicação (CIP)
(Câmara Brasileira do Livro, SP, Brasil)

Sasahara, Aline
   Fogo de Chão : Gaucho tradition gains worldwide status / Aline
Sasahara. -- São Paulo : Prêmio, 2010.

   ISBN: 85-8619345-3

   Bibliografia.

   1. Churrascaria Fogo de Chão - História 2. Família Coser - História 3.
Imigrantes italianos - Rio Grande do Sul - História I. Título.

10-05707   CDD-647.9509

Índices para catálogo sistemático:
   1. Churrascaria Fogo de Chão : História   647.9509
   2. Fogo de Chão : Churrascaria : História   647.9509

PHOTOGRAPHY CREDITS

Fogo de Chão Collection: pages 6, 7, 8, 9, 14, 30, 33, 34, 36, 37, 38, 42, 44, 45, 50, 51, 52, 53, 55, 60, 64 (left), 68, 69, 70, 71, 73, 76, 78, 79, 80, 81, 82, 83, 84, 85, 86, 87, 90, 91, 93, 94, 95 (right), 98, 99, 100, 101, 102, 103, 104, 105, 106, 108, 109, 110, 113 and back cover.

Family Coser Collection: pages 21, 23, 27, 29, 30 (top) and 31.

The Memorial of the Immigrant Collection: page 25.

ZEH Architecture Studio Collection: page 72.

Gladstone Campos: cover and pages 16, 17, 18, 19, 20, 22, 26, 28, 40, 41, 46, 47, 48, 49, 54, 56, 57, 58, 59, 61, 62, 64 (left), 65, 67, 74, 75, 88, 89, 92, 95 (left), 96, 111, 114, 115, 116, 117 (left).

Support: